Language and Being: An Analytic Phenomenology

LANGUAGE AND BEING:
AN ANALYTIC PHENOMENOLOGY

by Stephen A. Erickson

New Haven and London: Yale University Press 1970

Published with assistance from
the Mary Cady Tew Memorial Fund.

Library of Congress catalog card number: 74–99823
Standard book number: 300–01195–4
Designed by John O. C. McCrillis
set in Garamond type,
and printed in the United States of America by
The Carl Purington Rollins Printing-Office of
the Yale University Press, New Haven, Connecticut.
Distributed in Great Britain, Europe, Asia, and
Africa by Yale University Press Ltd., London; in
Canada by McGill-Queen's University Press, Montreal; and
in Mexico by Centro Interamericano de Libros
Académicos, Mexico City.

To W. T. J.

Preface

Thoreau is supposed to have said that the material men collect in their youth to build a bridge to the moon is used in middle age to build a woodshed. My material is a set of interrelated questions concerning language, meaning, and human worlds (forms of life). Whether answers to these questions assume the gestalt of a bridge or shed I am unable to say. I am convinced, however, that the questions are important to raise. It is my hope that others will aid in their pursuit—thus this book.

In thinking through and writing this study I have received help from a number of sources. I wish to thank Pomona College for a summer fellowship provided from a grant by the Ford Foundation to the Claremont Colleges, and for a research grant from funds for the development of the humanities provided jointly by the College and the Ford Foundation. Thanks are also due to the National Endowment for the Humanities, which awarded me a Summer Stipend for the summer of 1968 to pursue this study.

Small portions of this book have appeared in earlier versions in various journals: *Man and World* 1 (1968): 563–86; *Man and World* 2 (1969): 228–47; *Philosophy Forum* 7 (December 1968): 35–45; *The Review of Metaphysics* 19 (1966): 462–92. I wish to thank the editors of these journals for allowing me to use my materials in their altered form in this present volume, *Language and Being*.

A portion of this book has also appeared in earlier form in *New Essays in Phenomenology*, ed. James M. Edie (Chicago: Quadrangle Books, 1969), pp. 39–49.

A number of publishers and copyright holders have granted permission to quote materials.

Quotations from Wittgenstein's *Philosophical Investigations* appear by kind permission of Basil Blackwell on behalf of the executors of Ludwig Wittgenstein.

Quotations from Wittgenstein's *Tractatus Logico Philosophicus* appear by permission of the Humanities Press and Routledge and Kegan Paul, Ltd.

The two quotations from J. L. Austin's *Philosophical Papers* appear by permission of the Clarendon Press, Oxford.

The quotations from Heidegger's *An Introduction to Metaphysics,* translated by Ralph Manheim, appear by permission of Yale University Press.

Quotations from Heidegger's *Being and Time* appear by the very kind permission of Basil Blackwell and by permission of Harper & Row.

My colleague Morton Beckner and ex-colleague Robert Fogelin have provided me with valuable criticisms. Their help enabled me to avoid some serious mistakes.

With my wife Marty I shared experiences which made scholarship the servant of inquiry.

Finally, I am indebted to my friend and colleague W. T. Jones. Without his counsel this study might never have attained publishable form.

S.A.E.

Contents

Preface   vii

Abbreviations   x

Introduction   1

1 Being: A Linguistic Approach   4
2 The Meaning of Being   44
3 Phenomenology and Language   80
4 The Doctrine of Mediated Reflexivity   127

Index   163

Abbreviations

EIM   *Einführung in die Metaphysik*

ID   *Identität und Differenz*

IP   "In Search of Phenomenology"

KB   *Kant und Das Problem Der Metaphysik*

KdRv   *Kritik der Reinen Vernunft*

PI   *Philosophical Investigations*

SZ   *Sein und Zeit*

Introduction

The general theme of this study is rapprochement insofar as it bears upon the clarification and solution of contemporary philosophical problems. The specific problems with which it is concerned are located at the conceptual intersection of the following questions:

What is meaning?
What is the philosophical significance of language?
What is a (human) world?

These questions intersect in crucial ways and, taken together, belong to a realm of contemporary thought largely left uncharted by conceptual cartographers: the uneasy meeting place of the philosophy of language and philosophical anthropology. I hope to show precisely what is problematic about this region and to suggest the form in which a more penetrating philosophical investigation of it might be carried out. The former requires that I reformulate the questions stated above in more helpful ways; the latter, that I outline some methods to be employed in finding answers to them. Needless to say, these tasks are nearly the same.

As my major means to these ends I shall examine the relevant aspects of the philosophy of Heidegger. But my study is as much a selective examination of the so-called early Heidegger as it is a pursuit of the long-range goals I have just outlined. There are two reasons why I have chosen this means and then allowed it to become an end in its own right. First, the early Heidegger is to my knowledge the only contemporary philosopher who deals in a sustained and rigorous way with all three of the questions I have listed. Though I do not agree with many of his answers to these questions, I think Heidegger provides a model for understanding the questions in their conceptual interdependence. Much of the value of this model lies in its suggestiveness with respect to alternative models, and it is toward an articulation of a more adequate model that my efforts are ultimately directed. Heidegger's views thus provide a point of orientation from which to explore and map this rather difficult philosophical terrain.

Second, though I am addressing myself to philosophers of both phenomenological and analytical persuasion, my study is weighted slightly more toward the interests of analytic philosophers. By presenting some of Heidegger's views I hope to bring into relief some assumptions which I believe to be inherent in and especially problematic to analytic philosophy. Phenomenological philosophy's commitments on these same subjects are themselves often unexpressed, and in the course of presenting Heidegger's views I hope to bring these commitments into relief too. Because Heidegger has much to say about language and meaning, about human worlds and man, and because he is in important respects a representative phenomenologist, he is peculiarly suited for this attempt at double exposure. The comparisons which I engage in however are offered solely for the purpose of clarifying the questions I am attempting to reformulate.

Given my aims, my choice of means, and my conception of my audience, three consequences follow with respect to the development of my argument. The first is perhaps obvious. In discussing Heidegger I must sometimes assume the role of expositer and other times I must act as critic. Generally speaking, as the study progresses I move from exposition to criticism, though each of the four chapters will have elements of both. Second, in places where I consider it appropriate I modify Heidegger's views. The third consequence for my exposition follows more directly from the nature of the audience I hope to reach. Since I hope to count among my readers representatives of both major schools of contemporary Western philosophy, and since their vocabularies differ radically, I have been forced to make a number of choices along the way as to terminology. For the most part I recast Heidegger's views in the vocabulary of linguistic analysis. To bring Heidegger's views into relief I resort in some places to direct comparisons with views held by such philosophers as Wittgenstein, Austin, Merleau-Ponty, and Wilfred Sellars.

My study divides into four chapters. In the first two I discuss Heidegger's views on meaning. The primary considerations of the first chapter—Being: A Linguistic Approach—are the grammatical and etymological dimensions of Heidegger's analysis of the perplexing notion of Being. Here I try to determine the conceptual locus, if any, of Being as a philosophical problem. Since, as I point out, Being for Heidegger is undisclosed *meaning,* this discussion prepares the way for a more critical analysis of the concept of meaning in the second chapter—The Meaning of Being. At the end of this chapter I move from Heidegger through Ryle to a discussion and tentative reformulation of the first of my guiding questions:

What is meaning?

The third chapter—Phenomenology and Language—deals more directly with Heidegger's views on language. After a critical comparison of his views with those held by Wittgenstein, and a brief discussion of some nonetymological uses of language in the service of phenomenology, I conclude this chapter with a tentative reformulation of the second of my guiding questions:

What is the philosophical significance of language?

Since Heidegger's views on language and meaning are in an important and philosophically illuminating sense inseparable, the divisions between these first three chapters are very imperfect.

In the fourth and final chapter—The Doctrine of Mediated Reflexivity—I discuss, modify, and extend Heidegger's philosophical position concerning man and the worlds of man's experience. Here I tentatively reformulate the third of my guiding questions:

What is a (human) world?

CHAPTER 1

Being: A Linguistic Approach

I shall be concerned with the philosophy of Heidegger. More specifically, I shall be examining some of Heidegger's early views for the purpose of reformulating three important questions.

> What is meaning?
> What is the philosophical significance of language?
> What is a (human) world?

The specific problems presented by these questions, and their reformulation and interrelation, will be dealt with as they arise in the course of the study. Heidegger however presents a more pressing and immediate difficulty. He might in fact be termed a problem in his own right.

The "Heidegger problem" is this. Any attempt to discuss the philosophical work of Heidegger must face up to three hard facts, and in the end admit a fourth. First, many if not most Anglo–American philosophers do not take Heidegger seriously enough to bother to comprehend his thought, and, secondly, even those who take the time to study Heidegger's philosophical writings find his views so enigmatic as to be nearly impenetrable. The third fact is that Heidegger is in large measure responsible for this state of affairs. The fourth is that in spite of this Heidegger repays careful study.

Consider these remarks from the preface to the seventh (and subsequent) editions of *Being and Time*:

> While the previous editions have borne the designation "First Half," this has now been deleted. After a quarter of a century, the second half could no longer be added unless the first were to be presented anew. Yet the road it has taken remains even

today a necessary one, if our Dasein is to be stirred by the question of Being. For the elucidation of this question the reader may refer to my *An Introduction to Metaphysics*.[1]

The major issue which concerns Heidegger is the formulation of, and answer to, a deceptively simple question: What is the meaning of Being?[2] But both the force of this question, and what would constitute a plausible answer remain mysteries. If anyone were asked to state the meaning of the Being of an ashtray, an automobile, or himself, much less the meaning of Being as such, he would probably be at a loss to know what to say or what to look for. In this connection I shall turn to *An Introduction to Metaphysics*.[3] Here some valuable hints can be gathered about the puzzling question which Heidegger raises, the *Seinsfrage:*

What is the meaning of Being?

In this chapter I explore this question through a linguistic examination of the term 'Being' and its derivatives. This will involve a number of methodological considerations. In the next chapter I discuss the term 'meaning.' For Heidegger the question of the mean-

1. Martin Heidegger, *Sein und Zeit* (Tübingen, 1957), g.v, e.17. The English edition I refer to is the Macquarrie and Robinson translation, from which I have taken the wording for the quotations for this book. See *Being and Time*, trans. John Macquarrie and Edward Robinson (New York, 1962). Here and after I cite *Sein und Zeit* as SZ followed by the appropriate page numbers in the German (denoted by g.) and the English (denoted by e.) editions. 'Dasein' is a terminus technicus in Heidegger which is roughly equivalent to the term 'man.' I shall be discussing it at some length in chapter four.

2. The absence of single quotes around the term 'Being' is intentional. As will become clear shortly, Heidegger holds the view that Being itself has meaning, not simply the words through which reference to Being is made. This view is not altogether implausible. See pp. 44 ff.

3. Heidegger, *Einführung in die Metaphysik* (Tübingen, 1953). The English edition I refer to is the Manheim translation, from which, with a few minor revisions, I have taken the wording for the quotations for this book. See *An Introduction to Metaphysics*, trans. Ralph Manheim (Garden City, 1961). Hereafter I will cite *Einführung in die Metaphysik* as EIM followed by the appropriate page numbers in the German and the English editions.

ing of Being is a question concerning the meaning of meaning, and thus these first two chapters have as their task the clarification, criticism, and extension of Heidegger's views on the nature of meaning. At the end of the second chapter I define and discuss the "problem of meaning" independently of Heidegger's specific formulations and reformulate the question: What is meaning?

The crucial problem to consider in this first chapter, then, is what can be meant by 'Being.' If someone is asked what the color of a particular ashtray is, he knows how to go about answering. Color-talk is complex, but we know its rules. If, on the other hand, he is asked what the *Being* of that ashtray is, he would almost certainly be at a loss to know even what to look for. He might wonder whether or not he has heard the question correctly. In contrast to color-talk, the rules of Being-talk are anything but straightforward. One is tempted to call talk about Being nonsense.

Heidegger himself is not only aware of this line of thought but, with a few qualifications to be discussed later, he grants its validity. That 'Being' is an empty word for most if not all of us is taken for granted by Heidegger as the starting point of his investigation into the term[4]—an investigation which takes on an explicitly linguistic character in the second chapter of *An Introduction to Metaphysics*.[5]

According to Heidegger, 'Being'—*das Sein*—is derived from a particular verb form, the infinitive *(modus infinitivus)*. The term is therefore a verbal substantive such as, for example, dreaming, falling, smiling, and so on.[6]

German exhibits this derivation more perspicuously than does English. Take any infinitive, e.g. *'träumen'* (to dream), capitalize it, place the appropriate definitive article before it, and you have a verbal substantive, e.g. *'das Träumen'* (dreaming). In English, on the other hand, this transition involves a slightly more complicated operation. The infinitive prefix 'to' is dropped, and the gerund suffix 'ing' is added. In the case which concerns us we move from 'to be' to 'Being.' The reasons for capitalizing 'Being' and not other

4. SZ g.2, e.21.
5. EIM g.40–56, e.43–61.
6. EIM g.42–43, e.45–46.

verbal substantives—a common practice in studies of Heidegger written in English—are almost exclusively conventional in nature. Such capitalization serves to mark 'Being' as a technical term.

Verbal substantives typically refer to happenings; they refer to acts in the broad Aristotelian sense. Following Heidegger, I shall apply this interpretation to "Being," which Heidegger often refers to in post–*Being and Time* writings *as* a happening,[7] and think of Being therefore as an Aristotelian act.

Now consider the following statements.

> *Dreaming* is a means of maintaining sleep.
> *Falling* is a cause of disturbances in the inner ear.
> *Smiling* is often the best way of responding to an insult.

Obviously each is a perfectly normal statement which anyone would understand. The case of 'Being' is different, however, for what can be said about Being, granting even the added knowledge that it is to be thought of as a happening? How might one complete a sentence which began:

> *Being* is . . .

There would be something odd about any such statement. Heidegger is well aware of this too, and he sticks therefore to an analysis of infinitives, from which verbal substantives are derived.[8]

At this point Heidegger shifts from German to Greek.[9] A brief explanation of the rationale of this shift is required. Heidegger holds that, since Western philosophy had its genesis in Greek thought,[10] the basic notions in terms of which Western man philosophizes have grown (sometimes rather violently) out of the Greek language and have their roots in that language. The terms embodying these notions have been translated into Latin, and these eventually into German, French, and English. Heidegger concludes that, to be appreciated properly in their significance for philosophy,

7. See, for example, EIM g.153–54, e.168.
8. EIM g.43, e.46.
9. EIM g.43 ff., e.46 ff.
10. EIM g.10–11, e.11; g.75, e.83.

these terms must be understood in the light of the Greek language out of which they arose.[11] In particular, to discuss the philosophical significance of the concept of Being is to discover the origin and status of the term 'Being' as it arose within the language of the Greeks.

There is surely nothing particularly unorthodox about this view.[12] Wittgenstein, for example, states that a good way of coming to understand a word is by finding out how you would teach it to a child. Wittgenstein does not hold that words mean only what children understand them to mean nor that sophisticated or technical terminology is by its very nature to be distrusted. He simply implies that discovering how a word might be taught to a child is a good way of seeing how a word comes into actual use. And this helps us to understand the various extended, qualified, and sometimes technical roles that the word comes to play in the multiplicity of more sophisticated language games into which it enters.

Similarly Heidegger holds neither that philosophical terms mean only what the Greeks understood them to mean nor that German, French, and English philosophical terms and phraseology are inherently suspect. He implies rather that a careful examination of the context and circumstances out of which a term comes into actual use—here to be found in the appropriation and consequent modification of the Greek language by Greek philosophers—helps us understand the various extended, qualified, and almost always technical roles that that term comes to play in the rather highly developed contemporary language games into which it enters and thereby becomes a concern to us—in particular, in those played by German-, French-, and English-speaking philosophers.[13] Thus for Heidegger, to do philosophy is to concern oneself with the Greek language, though, to be sure, philosophy involves much more than this as well.

In Greek, as Heidegger points out, the fundamental form of the

11. EIM g.45, e.49.

12. In this connection, see pp. 14 ff.

13. Though this explanation of Heidegger's appeal to the Greek language should suffice for the present, it raises a cluster of problems concerning language. I shall concern myself with these problems in chapters two and three.

verb is the first person singular. The infinitive, the *modus infinitivus*, is a mode of this basic form. Now *'modus'* is the Latin translation for the Greek term 'ἔνκλισις' which means "deviation." More specifically it indicates a deviation from standing upright and straight in a determinate manner.[14] The infinitive thus represents a deviation. If verbal substantives are derived from infinitives, then, from the standpoint of Greek, 'Being' is derived from a "deviant" form of the verb.

'Deviation' has a slightly pejorative connotation. Heidegger traces 'Being' back to its origins in Greek speculative thought. But Heidegger also thinks Greeks went wrong in their formulation of the question of Being. The reconciliation of these two seemingly antagonistic beliefs, however, is not difficult. Heidegger's position is this: the Greeks determined the course of Western philosophical tradition by their formulations of various philosophical notions and problems. These notions and problems have been passed on as the substance of this tradition, passed on as much by seemingly inno- cent translations of the Greek philosophical vocabulary as by ex- plicit attempts—such as those of Aquinas, Leibniz and Hegel—to deal with issues raised by the Greeks. All attempts to philosophize, therefore, inevitably fall under the influence of Greek ways of thought. But Heidegger does not hold that the Greek formulations need be accepted as they present themselves. On the other hand, to free oneself from the covert influence of Greek models, one must recognize that one is under the influence of those models and under- stand their nature and the commitments they carry with them.

> Greek ontology and its history—which, in their numerous filiations and distortions, determine the conceptual character of philosophy even today—prove that when Dasein under- stands either itself or Being in general, it does so in terms of the "world," and that the ontology which has thus arisen has deteriorated to a tradition in which it gets reduced to some- thing self-evident. . . . If the question of Being is to have its own history made transparent, then this hardened tradition must be loosened up, and the concealments which it has

14. EIM g.43–49, e.48–53.

brought about must be dissolved. We understand this task as one in which by taking the *question of Being as our clue,* we are to *destroy* the traditional content of ancient ontology until we arrive at those primordial experiences in which we achieved our first ways of determining the nature of Being—the ways which have guided us ever since.

In thus demonstrating the origin of our basic ontological concepts by an investigation in which their "birth certificate" is displayed, we have nothing to do with a vicious relativizing of ontological standpoints. But this destruction is just as far from having the *negative* sense of shaking off the ontological tradition. We must, on the contrary, stake out the positive possibilities of that tradition, and this always means keeping it within its limits.[15]

Consider now three points about infinitives. First, they do not indicate person, number, voice, mood, or tense. Thus the "deviation" is toward indeterminacy. Second, the infinitive is an abstract and late verb form.[16] Finally, Heidegger thinks of it as naming "something which underlies all the inflections of the verb,"[17] and thereby assigns to it a metalinguistic as opposed to an "object language" function,[18] namely, the function of referring to the terms 'is,' 'am,' 'are,' and so on. In any case, the *modus infinitivus* is the mode of unlimitedness and indeterminateness, in contrast to the *modus finitus,* the mode of limitation and determinateness of verbal signification.[19]

Granting that the infinitive deviates toward indeterminacy, what can be concluded, Heidegger asks rhetorically, but that the verbal substantive merely stabilizes this emptiness by offering itself as a term through which reference to the emptiness can be secured? Moreover,

15. SZ g.21–23, e.43–44.
16. EIM g.51–52, e.55–56.
17. EIM g.52, e.57.
18. I shall be taking up this metalinguistic function of the infinitive on pp. 13 ff. and therefore postpone any discussion of it until then.
19. EIM g.45, e.48.

The transformation of the infinitive into a verbal substantive further stabilizes as it were the emptiness that already resided in the infinitive; *'sein'* is set down like a stable object. The substantive *'Sein'* (Being) implies that what has thus been named itself "is." Now Being itself becomes something that "is," . . . Can it now surprise us that 'Being' should be so empty a word when the very word form is based on an emptying and an apparent stabilization of emptiness? Let this word 'Being' be a warning to us. Let us not be lured into the emptiest of all forms, the verbal substantive.[20]

If one takes seriously Heidegger's suggestion of the metalinguistic role played by infinitives, it looks as if asking the question of Being is an invitation to disaster. It creates the illusion of an object, whose nature in turn is best defined by its tendency toward vacuity.

Somewhat paradoxically, however, Heidegger applies this conclusion not to his own work but only to the philosophical tradition which precedes him. He maintains the validity of the question concerning Being in the face of his own criticism of the term 'Being' and the philosophical tendencies to which use of this term gives rise.

Toward the philosophy that has preceded him, however, Heidegger is by no means as charitable. He is as hard on previous philosophers as his Anglo–American contemporaries are on him. According to Heidegger, the Western philosophical tradition has tended to view Being as an object or entity.[21] Further, because of the strong influence of Christian theology on this tradition, Being has usually been considered to be the highest or supreme entity.[22] Such thinking, Heidegger believes, was based on the tendency of Greek philosophers to formulate the problem of Being in a certain way, misconstrue the import of the formulation, and then fall under the influence of a certain linguistic model.[23] Its inevitable outcome

20. EIM g.52–53, e.57.
21. In this connection see SZ g.6–7, e.25–26. See also Heidegger, "The Way Back into the Ground of Metaphysics," trans. Walter Kaufmann in *Existentialism from Dostoevsky to Sartre,* ed. Walter Kaufmann (New York, 1959), pp. 207–21. See especially p. 218.
22. SZ g.6–7, e.25–26.
23. EIM g.38 ff., e.41 ff.

was Nietzsche's conclusion that Being is a vacuous vapor[24]—a
conclusion prepared by Hegel in his discussion of the "dialectical"
relation obtaining between Being and Nothing, which appears at
the beginning of the Jena Logic.[25] Early in *Being and Time* Heidegger writes:

> The Being of entities "is" not itself an entity. If we are to
> understand the problem of Being, our first philosophical step
> consists in not μυθον τινα διηγεισθαι in not "telling a
> story"—that is to say, in not defining entities as entities by
> tracing them back in their origin to some other entities, as if
> Being had the character of some possible entity.[26]

But, granting that the tradition has made this mistake, what about
Heidegger himself? Heidegger charges that the concept of Being
is vacuous. To avoid this result one must, it would seem, at least be
aware of the temptation to reify, together with its attendant dangers.
The question is whether or not having such an awareness will be
sufficient as a means of avoiding the unwanted result: an ascription
of vacuity to the concept of Being. The matter is made even more
difficult. Heidegger also charges that, apart even from the results of
transforming an infinitive into a verbal substantive, there is already
a tendency toward emptiness of content in the very infinitive
itself[27]—a criticism which cuts more deeply and appears to be
more difficult to answer.

Here it is Heidegger's conviction that the Greeks formulated the
question of Being in terms of the infinitive because of their concern
with the general understood generically as opposed to the particular.[28] If the infinitive is thought to name "something which underlies all the inflections of the verb," then resorting to the infinitive
might well be a quest for some sort of generic commonality in-

24. EIM g.27–28, e.29–30.

25. Georg Wilhelm Friedrich Hegel, *Wissenschaft der Logik* (Hamburg,
1963), g.66–95, e.94–120. The English edition I refer to is the Johnston
and Struthers translation. See *Science of Logic, trans.* W. H. Johnston and
L. G. Struthers (London, 1961).

26. SZ g.6, e.26. (The Greek reference is to Plato, *Sophist* 242c.)

27. EIM g.51–53, e.55–57.

28. Ibid.; see also SZ g.3, e.22–23.

volved in referring to things merely insofar as they *are*—which is to say, again in the phraseology belonging to the philosophical tradition, insofar as they have Being. Heidegger clearly rejects this line of reasoning. The quest for generic commonality is viewed by him to be fundamentally misguided. He writes:

> The "universality" of Being is not that of a *class* or *genus*. The term 'Being' does not define that realm of entities which is uppermost when these are articulated conceptually according to genus and species: οὔτε τò ὄν γένος.[29]

Heidegger does not take exception to the use of the infinitive '*sein*' itself—notwithstanding its presumed tendencies toward emptiness. He objects, rather, to the attempt to put the infinitive in the service of the quest for generic commonality.[30] The tendencies of the infinitive toward emptiness are viewed by Heidegger merely as tendencies. To avoid their realization and to pursue the question of Being further he resorts to an etymological study of the crucial infinitive, '*sein*' (to be).[31]

I must here say a word concerning Heidegger's view that '*sein*' serves a metalinguistic function. If this is ever true, it is clearly not always true. When I say, 'that is one thing I do not want *to be*,' the infinitive is functioning in a straightforward and unmetalinguistic manner. Examples of this sort can be multiplied indefinitely. But what Heidegger has in mind is something like the following.

"Being," he writes, "is always the Being of an entity."[32] We refer to entities and their characteristics in a variety of different ways, depending usually upon what sort of information we intend to convey. I say "usually" here to allow for the fact that information-giving is but one of the purposes served in such referring contexts. Now a standard means of referring is the declarative sentence.

29. SZ g.3, e.22. (The Greek reference here is to Aristotle, *Metaphysics* B3. 998b22.)

30. EIM g.42–54, e.46–58.

31. EIM g.54–56, e.58–61. Heidegger's etymological appeals are sometimes confined to German, sometimes to Greek. I have more to say about this curious fact shortly.

32. SZ g.9, e.29.

When we want to identify an object for someone, we say that it is an ashtray; when we want to identify its color, we say that it is blue. But how do we refer to its Being? Heidegger thinks that declarative sentences (as well as other kinds of sentences) constantly refer to this "aspect" of entities. The major means by which this reference is secured, Heidegger thinks, is the copula.[33] Thus, if we say that the sky is blue, 'is' indicates the sky's Being. If we say that we are tired, 'are' refers to our Being. Heidegger writes at one point,

> We can . . . [and, in effect, must] define . . . the ontological meaning of the 'is,' which a superficial theory of propositions and judgments has deformed to a mere "copula."[34]

Now if Being is always the Being of an entity, and entities are of such a nature as to be referred to as I's, we's, you's, he's, she's, it's, and they's, Being must then be referred to straightforwardly by 'am's,' 'are's,' and 'is's.' Given this position, what is needed is a means of referring to these last three terms and, indirectly, to that which is referred to through their employment. It is here that Heidegger relies on the metalinguistic function of the infinitive.[35]

We must now turn to the question of etymologies. To maintain the validity of the question of Being in the face of objections he himself formulates, Heidegger turns to the etymology of the infinitive *'sein.'* This raises an obvious question: What is the significance of an etymological appeal in philosophy? This is worth pausing to consider.

In "A Plea For Excuses" Austin writes:

> I will mention two points of method which are, experience has convinced me, indispensable aids . . .
>
> One is that a word never—well, hardly ever—shakes off its etymology and its formation. In spite of all changes in and extensions of and additions to its meanings, and indeed rather pervading and governing these, there will still persist the old idea . . .

33. EIM g.23 ff., e.25 ff.; SZ g.4, e.23.
34. SZ g.349, e.400–01.
35. This point is clearly a matter of interpretation. For a discussion of some of the issues which surround the question, see pp. 22 ff.

And the second point is connected with this. Going back into the history of a word, very often into Latin, we come back pretty commonly to pictures or *models* . . . a model must be recognized for what it is . . . the word [the particular word Austin has in mind here is 'causing'] snares us: we are struggling to ascribe to it a new unanthropomorphic meaning, yet constantly, in search for its analysis, we unearth and incorporate the lineaments of the ancient model . . . Examining such a word historically, we may well find that it has been extended to cases that have by now too tenuous a relation to the model case, that it is a source of confusion and superstition.

There is too another danger in words that invoke models half forgotten or not. It must be remembered that there is no necessity whatsoever that the various models used in creating our vocabulary, primitive or recent, should all fit together neatly as parts into one single, total model or scheme . . . It is possible, and indeed highly likely, that our assortment of models will include some, or many, that are overlapping, conflicting, or more generally simply *disparate*.[36]

At this point Austin adds in a footnote:

This is by way of a general warning in philosophy. It seems to be too readily assumed that if we can only discover the true meanings of each of a cluster of key terms, usually historic terms, that we use in some particular field . . . then it must without question transpire that each will fit into place in some single, interlocking, consistent, conceptual scheme. Not only is there no reason to assume this, but all historical probability is against it, especially in the case of a language derived from such various civilizations as ours is.[37]

I have quoted Austin at such length because of his close connection with, yet at the same time definitive divergence from, Heidegger with respect to the methodological commitments of etymological analysis. Heidegger would agree with Austin that a word

36. J. L. Austin, *Philosophical Papers,* ed. J. C. Urmson and G. J. Warnock (Oxford, 1961), pp. 149–51.
37. Ibid., p. 151.

(almost) never frees itself completely from its etymological ancestry. Therefore, to discover the force of a term employed in philosophy it is necessary to ascertain its lineage—an exercise in linguistic history and logical geography.[88] As Heidegger sees the matter, this means tracing the term back into Greek in most, if not all, instances.

> Like all other Latin grammatical terms, this term [*modus infinitivus*] stems from the work of the Greek grammarians. Here again we run into the process of translation which we have mentioned in connection with the word 'φύσις'. We need not go into the details here of how grammar arose among the Greeks, how it was taken over by the Romans and handed on to the Middle Ages and the modern era. In regard to this history of grammar we know a good many details. So far there is no work that really penetrates this process, so fundamental to the establishment and formation of all Western spirit. We even lack an adequate formulation of the problems underlying such a study, which must inevitably be undertaken one day, remote as this whole matter may seem from current interests.

> What gives this development its entire meaning is that Western grammar sprang from the reflection of the Greeks on the Greek language.[39]

> ... the manner in which the Greeks understood ... [entities in their Being] was bound to make itself felt in their view and definition of language. Only on this basis can we understand these terms which, as mood and case, have long become threadbare and meaningless for us.

> In this lecture we shall always be coming back to the Greeks' view of Being, because this view, though totally banalized and unrecognized as Greek, is still the prevailing Western view. Since this is true not only in regard to the doctrines of philosophy but in the most common and everyday matters, we shall attempt, as we examine the Greek view of language, to characterize the first fundamentals of the Greek view of Being.

38. EIM g.42 ff., e.45 ff.
39. EIM g.43, e.46–47.

This method is chosen intentionally. We hope to show by an example drawn from grammar that the determining Western experience, idea, and interpretation of language have grown out of a very definite understanding of Being.[40]

Critics of analytic philosophy often charge that grammatical features of English are put in the service of covert metaphysical biases and used as criteria to exclude various topics from discussion. One might level the same charge against Heidegger with much greater justice. Heidegger often appeals not to the Greek derivation of a word, but only to its German antecedents.[41] In doing this he comments that Greek and German are the two most spiritual of languages and that to do philosophy is to be bound up in one or both of them.[42]

How can one justify the elevation of German to such a position of revelatory preeminence? Were one forced to defend this position, one's reply, I think, would fall into two parts.[43] In the first place, one would have to insist that for a German no other language could be appreciated and employed subtly, sensitively, and deftly enough to do the philosophical work that can be done by and in German. A second line of argument might be that there are certain philosophical problems that have their genesis in German, its unique characteristics, idiosyncracies, and the particular way in which it has been appropriated by German philosophers. The difficulty with both these replies is that they defend the original claim concerning the "spirituality" and the philosophical preeminence of the German language by nearly qualifying that claim out of existence. One cannot but think that the spirit of German nationalism rather than either of these more reasoned and measured replies represents Heidegger's primary and most compelling reason for his remarks concerning the German language.

40. EIM g.45, e.49.
41. See, for example, SZ g.54, e.79–80.
42. EIM g.43, e.47.
43. Here, obviously, I am called upon to interpret rather than merely to explicate. To my knowledge Heidegger offers no defense of his position in any of his writings.

Heidegger agrees, then, with Austin that a word (almost) never frees itself completely from its etymological ancestry. For Heidegger, however, the "tracing back" that this entails for philosophy is a tracing back into Greek and sometimes into German—seldom if ever into Latin, which is more often Austin's inclination. If the appeal to Greek is often justified, the appeal to German is usually methodologically suspect.

Heidegger would certainly agree with Austin that models often exercise a covert control over our thinking, and therefore that certain words—ones that derive their force from these models—"snare us."[44] In particular, Heidegger holds that we are ensnared by a certain model for the understanding of Being.[45] This model has been drawn from the realm of time.

On Heidegger's analysis, though Being is not itself an entity, it is always the Being *of* an entity. Let me now add that every entity has Being.[46] By 'entity' Heidegger would mean any something, a term for which could properly stand in the subject place in a simple subject-predicate judgment. Presumably this takes in such diverse items as persons, porridge bowls, petitions for cloture, poverty, pique, and Mr. Pickwick, not to mention others. Roughly speaking, then, the category of "entity" would correspond to Kant's category of "substance"—with the added Aristotelian qualification that a substance cannot be predicated any other place.

Now *if* every entity has Being, and *if* we are ensnared by a certain model for the understanding of Being, this model takes on considerable importance, for it partly determines our understanding of every entity we experience. Because it is so pervasive, the model must be difficult to grasp. In fact, one is tempted to think, if the matter gets any attention at all, that there is no model employed whatsoever. This is an obvious consequence of the fact that in its very pervasiveness there would be nothing with which the model could be compared. The temptation is to think that Being is under-

44. See, for instance, SZ g.53–54, e.79.
45. SZ g.2, e.21.
46. To my knowledge Heidegger never makes this point explicitly. It is obviously essential to his philosophy however, particularly in the light of the Kantian dimensions of the philosophy.

stood in itself for what it is—if there truly *is* anything to understand in this regard. Heidegger wants to do two things in this connection. First, he wants to acquaint his readers with the model which holds them captive, and thereby free them from its total domination.[47] Second, he wants to present an alternative model, one free of the limitations he ascribes to the present one.

In this respect Heidegger's approach contrasts sharply with Austin's professed pluralism. Heidegger is willing to grant the existence of a variety of different models for understanding a variety of different things. Nonetheless, he thinks that all these models— and here we are talking about models employed overtly or covertly in Western philosophy—are determined in a very basic way by the one model by means of which Being is understood. While Austin is concerned to point out the various, probably conflicting or at least disparate, models which determine our thinking, Heidegger is concerned primarily about *one* model. This model is not viewed as being in conflict with other models; it is viewed, rather, as determinative of them in some basic way. Models other than that employed for understanding Being may well conflict with one another. In at least one respect, however, they are in harmony: they all do involve the same understanding of Being. It is this understanding and the model it employs, then, that serve as the focus of Heidegger's etymological analysis of 'Being' and its derivatives. And the goal of these analyses is much less descriptive than revisionary.[48]

Finally, while Austin stresses the variety of sources from which a language such as ours is derived and concludes in part from this that the chances of etymological analysis yielding consistent, interlocking conceptual schemes are slim, Heidegger takes an almost diametrically opposed course. He insists on the overwhelming primacy of one source, the Greek language, for understanding the various problems and models ingredient in contemporary philosophical discussions. Furthermore he thinks that a careful examination of various key terms in Greek or German will yield a consistent conceptual framework for comprehending explicitly the one

47. SZ g.21–22, e.43–44.
48. SZ g.17–19, e.39–40; see also SZ g.2–3, e.21–22.

model that the Western tradition has so far developed for understanding Being.[49]

To turn now to etymology proper: according to Heidegger, the inflections of *'sein'* are determined in their entirety by three different stems. I think it essential to quote Heidegger at length here:

> The first two stems to be named are Indo–European and also occur in the Greek and Latin words for 'Being.'
>
> 1. The oldest, the actual radical word is *'es,'* Sanskrit *'asus,'* life, the living, that which from out of itself stands and which moves and rests in itself: the self-standing [*Eigenständig*].
>
> To this radical belong in Sanskrit the verbal formations *'esmi,' 'esi,' 'esti,' 'asmi,'* to which correspond the Greek 'ἐιμι' and 'ἐιναι' the Latin *'esum'* and *'esse.' 'Sunt,' 'sind,'* and *'sein'* belong together. It is noteworthy that the *'ist'* has maintained itself in all Germanic languages from the very start (*'estin,' 'est'* ...).
>
> 2. The other Indo-European radical is *'bhu,' 'bheu.'* To it belong the Greek 'φυω,' to emerge, to be powerful, of itself to come to stand and remain standing. Up until now this *'bhu'* has been interpreted according to the usual superficial view of 'φυσις' and 'φυειν' as nature and "to grow." A more fundamental exegesis, stemming from preoccupation with the beginning of Greek philosophy, shows the "growing" to be an "emerging," which in turn is defined by presence and appearance. Recently the root 'φυ' has been connected with 'φα-φαινεσθαι.' Φυσις would then be that which emerges into the light, 'φυειν' would mean to shine, to give light and therefore to appear ...
>
> From this stem come the Latin perfect *'fui,' 'fuo,'* similarly our German *'bin,' 'bist,' 'wir birn,' 'ihr birt'* (which died out in the fourteenth century). The imperative *'bis'* (*'bis mein Weib,'* be my wife) survived longer.

---

49. Unfortunately Heidegger does not discuss the relation between Greek and German or assign a priority.

3. The third stem occurs only in the inflection of the Germanic verb *'sein'*: *'wes'*; Sanskrit: *'vasami'*; Germanic: *'wesan,'* to dwell, to sojourn; to *'ves'* belong: *'Festia,'* *'Fasti,'* *'Vesta,'* *'vestibulum.'* The German forms resulting from this stem are *'gewesen,'* *'was,'* *'war,'* *'es,'* *'west,'* *'wesen.'* The participle *'wesend'* is still preserved in *'anwesend'* [present] and *'abwesend'* [absent]. The substantive *'Wesen'* did not originally mean "whatness," quiddity, but enduring as presence, presence and absence. The *'sens'* in the Latin *'prae-sens'* and *'ab-sens'* has been lost . . .

From the three stems we derive the three initial concrete meanings: to live, to emerge, to linger or endure. These are established by linguistics, which also establishes that these initial meanings are extinct today, that only an "abstract" meaning, "to be," has been preserved.[50]

Etymologically, then, if Heidegger is correct, the word *'sein'*— the *modus infinitivus*—means something which is a mixture of three elements: to live, to emerge, and to linger or endure. Heidegger finds no indication, however, of how these meanings hang together.[51] Given the knowledge of these three meanings, the question of the meaning of Being takes the following form: What is the meaning of that happening, not itself an entity but in some way akin to something living, emerging, and enduring, which happens only with respect to entities and happens with respect to every entity? I say "akin to" to indicate the partially revisionary as opposed to descriptive intent of the etymological analysis.

As matters now stand, the situation with respect to Heidegger's leading question is still unclear. The meaning of the word 'Being' remains indeterminate, even after etymological analysis. If anything, in fact, the term 'Being' gives the appearance of having resulted from grammatical gymnastics performed on a mere copula. It is saved from total vacuity—and the surgical techniques em-

---

50. EIM g.54–55, e.58–59. I have chosen to rearrange single and double quotes and italicization to some extent here for purposes of clarity. (Note the curious use of both German and Greek in these analyses.)

51. EIM g.54–56, e.59–60.

ployed appear to be at best palliative—only by some ingenious etymological findings. These "findings," it should be added, are viewed by many philologists as highly suspect. Heidegger admits as much in a slightly different context:

> In the perspective of the common and prevailing definitions, in the perspective of modern and contemporary metaphysics, theory of knowledge, anthropology and ethics . . . our interpretation . . . must appear to be an arbitrary distortion. We are accused of reading into it things that an "exact interpretation" can never determine. This is true. In the usual present-day view what has been said here is a mere product of the farfetched and one-sided Heideggerian method of exegesis, which has already become proverbial.[52]

Having admitted all this, however, Heidegger continues to maintain that we do understand Being[53] and that we are constantly differentiating it from absence of Being. This understanding is (to use a phenomenological term) nonthematic, i.e. it is not an explicit, systematic, and conceptually articulated understanding.[54] Rather, Heidegger holds, it is a comprehension of Being indicated only by the ability we have to use the word 'is' and closely related terms.[55] As I have indicated, Heidegger holds that the (misconstrued) copula and related expressions have referring functions with respect to Being. It is this assertion that must now be looked into a little more closely.

Heidegger offers us a number of statements which, he claims, embody this peculiar referring function. Among them are the following:

(1) The lecture *is* in the auditorium.
(2) This man *is* from Swabia.
(3) The cup *is* of silver.
(4) The book *is* mine.

52. EIM g.134, e.147.
53. SZ g.5–6, e.25.
54. SZ g.363–64, e.414–15; g.5–6, e.25.
55. EIM g.23 ff., e.25 ff.

(5) Red *is* the port side.
(6) God *is*.
(7) The earth *is*.

To be sure, (6) and (7) are a bit odd; the others, however, are quite ordinary. Heidegger gives a partial interpretation of the 'is' in each of them.

(1) takes place
(2) comes (from)
(3) (is) made of
(4) belongs to
(5) stands for
(6) (is) really present
(7) (is) permanently there

Heidegger claims that, taken together, these indicate the sphere of actuality and presence, permanence and duration, abiding and occurrence. Clearly the conceptual meaning and (nongeneric) unity of these latter notions is problematic and in no small degree opaque. Nonetheless for Heidegger they evidence a genuine comprehension of Being, a nonthematic understanding in need of clarification and (ultimately) revision. Heidegger thinks of this understanding as the ordinary man's muted answer to the question of Being.

Now it is not altogether implausible to suppose that

The lecture is in the auditorium.

is at least roughly synonymous with

The lecture takes place in the auditorium.

Furthermore, whereas 'takes place' can be substituted for 'is' in this sentence with little if any loss of meaning, perhaps even a gain in clarity, 'takes place' could not be properly substituted for any other 'is' in the list. Heidegger appears to hold that the term 'is' in this sentence just *means* "takes place." (Since 'takes place,' of course, requires further philosophical attention in its own right, this last statement does not terminate analysis.) Since 'takes place' is not substitutable for any 'is' in the other sentences, according to

Heidegger's reasoning 'is' must have at least one (and as a matter of fact a number of) other meanings.[56]

> What cannot be argued away . . . is that the 'is' in our discourse manifests a rich diversity of meanings. In each one of these meanings we say the 'is' without, either before or afterward, effecting a special exegesis of 'is,' let alone reflecting on Being. The 'is,' meant now so and now so, simply wells up as we speak. Yet the diversity of its meanings is not arbitrary diversity.[57]

This is to say that 'is' is not a univocal term—it is more than a mere copula and its equivocity requires careful study. With this view I concur.

Though philosophically important, this study has been for the most part ignored by other philosophers. The reasons for this state of affairs are relatively simple. First, from a logical point of view —and here one has in mind the translation of sentences into symbolic notation by the use of quantification devices and so on— the 'is' can be taken to function as a copula in every case. Heidegger himself does not deny that in each use of the 'is' a "copulatic," a "bringing together," function is served. He does take exception to the suggestion that a grasp of this formally manageable lowest common denominator is sufficient for understanding the 'is' and that the 'is' therefore presents no problem.

> Regardless of how we interpret these examples, they show one thing clearly: in the 'is' Being discloses itself to us in a diversity of ways. Once again the assertion, which at first seemed plausible, that Being is an empty word is shown—more compellingly than ever—to be untrue . . . the 'is' in our discourse manifests a rich diversity of meanings.[58]

There is a second and more obvious reason why so many philosophers have ignored the 'is.' Paradoxically the study of the 'is' leads away from itself toward its context and to the elements that

56. EIM g.67–69, e.74–77.
57. EIM g.69, e.76.
58. EIM g.68–69, e.76.

in a formal sense it connects. On Heidegger's view this has its counterpart "outside" of the linguistic order. (I hedge 'outside' with double quotation marks because of Heidegger's complicated views about the relation between language and the so-called real order.) Heidegger states that Being is always the Being of an entity and that it can be comprehended only through an examination of entities, a remark which states in the material mode of speech roughly this same point.[59]

A final reason for ignoring the 'is' results from a group of factors conspiring together: the large number of contexts into which the 'is' enters, its seemingly insignificant role, and its highly multiple equivocity which gives it the appearance of being a univocal term.

One final set of linguistic considerations is relevant to our discussion of the term 'Being.' Though Heidegger's etymological concern goes via the route of the infinitive to the verbal substantive, and though with respect to ordinary language he places the problem of Being in the copula, yet in *Being and Time* he introduces his problem to his reader by reference to the present participle. Here he quotes from the *Sophist:*

> "For manifestly you have been long aware of what you mean when you use the expression *being.* We, however, who used to think we understood it, have now become perplexed."

> Do we in our time have an answer to the question of what we really mean by the word 'being?' Not at all. So it is fitting that we should raise anew *the question of the meaning of Being.*[60]

It is certainly ironic that a book so maligned for its abuse of grammar and its exotic terminology should begin with a linguistic consideration. But this particular linguistic consideration is

59. In this connection, see Rudolf Carnap, *The Logical Syntax of Language,* trans. Amethe Smeaton (Countess von Zeppelin) (Patterson, 1959), pp. 237 ff.

60. SZ g.2, e.19. Heidegger translates the present participle ὄv by the present participle of the verb *'sein': 'seiend.'* In the Macquarrie and Robinson translation *'seiend'* is translated, as in this passage, by the present participle 'being.'

neither arbitrarily chosen nor merely illustrative. On the contrary, the appeal to participles and participial constructions is in many ways the most crucial element in the constitution of the problem as Heidegger sees it. To see this we must have recourse to Kant and to some reflections on ordinary grammar.

For the modern tradition in philosophy prior to Kant, judgment is understood in a straightforward and perhaps naïvely simple way —if it comes under consideration at all. A judgment is a complex idea; ideas are combined to form complexes by conjunction; such complex ideas differ from judgments, if they differ at all, only in their force—for instance, in their lesser vivacity for Hume, in their not having gained the assent of the will for Descartes.

Kant modifies this view radically. For him the unity of a judgment is a basic and irreducible mode of unity. This unity cannot be built from elements with a cognitive unity of their own, outside of the judgment, which come together to constitute the judgment in its complexity. Rather, the unity of the judgment is fundamental. It can never be decomposed. From it one can only abstract.[61]

It follows for Kant that judgment is basic to the very "having" of ideas. Basic to and presupposed by our having the idea of red, for instance, is our having the idea of something's *being* red. It is here, then, that the participle 'being' enters in.

61. Wittgenstein holds roughly the same view, of course, as witnessed by his insistence that objects are dependent upon, and only have existence within, atomic states of affairs, and correspondingly that atomic propositions are the basic units of knowledge and meaning. Note his remarks on these matters in Ludwig Wittgenstein, *Tractatus Logico Philosophicus,* trans. D. F. Pears and B. F. McGuinness (London, 1963). Hereafter cited as *Tractatus.*

> The world is the totality of facts, not of things. (1.1).
> What is the case—a fact—is the existence of states of affairs. (2).
> A state of affairs (a state of things) is a combination of objects (things). (2.01).
> Things are independent insofar as they can occur in all *possible* situations, but this form of independence is a form of connexion with states of affairs, a form of dependence. (It is impossible for words to appear in two different rôles: by themselves, and in propositions.) (2.0122).
> Only propositions have sense; only in the nexus of a proposition does a name have meaning. (3.3).

It is by no means a controversial interpretation of Kant to say that for him knowledge is in large measure conceptual and that the conceptual structure of knowledge can be derived from a study of language. In the *Prolegomena,* Kant writes:

> To search in our daily cognition for the concepts, which do not rest upon particular experience, and yet occur · in all cognition of experience, where they as it were constitute the mere form of connection, presupposes neither greater reflection nor deeper insight, than to detect in a language the rules of the actual use of words generally, and thus to collect elements for a grammar. In fact both researches are very nearly related.[62]

Thus, repeating our example, to have the idea of something's *being* red for Kant is to have at one's disposal at least the pure concepts of substance and accident, and of course the empirical concept of red. In short, what is presupposed here is our having the *concept* of something's being red, which involves a battery of closely related concepts and is itself analyzable into a set of constituent concepts. For Heidegger what is presupposed in particular is one's having at one's disposal the (constituent) concept of Being, which is indicated by the term 'being.'[63]

Now for Kant concepts are incomplete judgments, existing only in the forms of judgment. This doctrine is perhaps best explained by an example. The concept of material body satisfies the following condition, which both defines it and serves as a criterion for determining whether the concept is being employed: a term referring to or indicating a particular item which falls within the concept's scope can stand in the subject place in a subject-predicate judgment and necessarily stands in the subject place when certain sorts of predicates stand in the predicate place. Since the concept of material body is an empirical concept, the question of which sorts of predicates entail its employment is empirical. On the other

62. Immanuel Kant, *Prolegomena to Any Future Metaphysics,* trans. Lewis White Beck (New York, 1950), p. 70. Flew quotes this passage in *Essays in Conceptual Analysis,* ed. Antony Flew (London, 1956), p. v. The quotation is Flew's translation.

63. SZ g. 1 ff., e.19 ff.

hand categories or *pure* concepts—as opposed to empirical concepts—exclude altogether references to empirical content. They are concepts of the very forms of judgment themselves and are thus second-order in nature. In short, they give us information concerning the forms which any judgment must take. The concept of substance, for example, is the concept of that which belongs in or can be fitted into the subject place of a subject-predicate judgment. To say of Socrates, then, that he is a substance is to say that the term 'Socrates' can be fitted into the subject place in an assertive judgment. The concept of cause is the concept of that which belongs to or can be fitted into the antecedent in an implication—leaving aside the problem of schematization. And so on.

But given this Kantian model what can be said of the concept of Being? It is at least safe to say that Heidegger views it as a *pure* concept.[64] Among other things he indicates that it is "transcendental for every entity."[65] Beyond this, however, Heidegger's position is difficult to puzzle out. Let me state in a formal mode of speech[66] what appears to be the major point concerning the concept: the concept refers to the pure form of connection which holds together, yet articulates, the various structural ingredients of statements in their formal (as opposed to their empirical) constitution. To say that Being is not itself an entity, then, is at least to say that the pure form of connection is not itself just another item. Were it so, it would fall prey to a number of Bradley's paradoxes. In particular, a regress would be started: one would be faced with the problem of connecting the form of connection with the items which it connects, and so on.

Provided that the formal mode of speech is retained, the closest analogue in contemporary philosophy to this concept of Being may well be Wittgenstein's notion of logical form. In the *Tractatus* he says:

64. SZ g.11, e.31.
65. SZ g.153, e.194–95.
66. Since language for Heidegger is the "House of Being," anything true about Being ought to be reflected in the structure and function of language. This, I think, is the justification for resorting at times to the formal mode of speech. See n. 59, above.

Propositions can represent the whole of reality, but they cannot represent what they must have in common with reality in order to be able to represent it—logical form.

In order to be able to represent logical form, we should have to be able to station ourselves with propositions somewhere outside logic, that is to say outside the world. (4.12)

Propositions cannot represent logical form: it is mirrored in them.

What finds its reflection in language, language cannot represent.

What expresses *itself* in language, *we* cannot express by means of language.

Propositions *show* the logical form of reality.

They display it. (4.121)

In style, problem orientation, and substance Wittgenstein and Heidegger are in most ways far apart. Nonetheless, Heidegger would subscribe wholeheartedly to the view expressed in the second sentence of 4.12. His way of making this point would be different of course. Here is one of his characteristic statements.

If the basic conditions which make interpretation possible are to be fulfilled, this must rather be done by not failing to recognize beforehand the essential conditions under which it can be performed. What is decisive is not to get out of the circle but to come into it in the right way. This circle of understanding is not an orbit in which any random kind of knowledge may move; it is the expression of the existential fore-structure of Dasein itself.[67]

What is perhaps more revealing is that the business of Heidegger's philosophical method—phenomenology, which I shall discuss at length in the third chapter—is to bring Being to *show* itself. What makes it difficult for Being to show itself is language.

67. SZ g.153, e.194–95.

There is a strange formula, seldom expressed, which has captivated the German philosophical mind from Leibniz through the rise of German idealism and even up to the present day: to be is to be determinate. I mention this as the first step in my transition from quasi-formal modes of speech, a transition which will go the way of unpacking this peculiar philosophical slogan.

German philosophers have worried much more perhaps than other philosophers about the way in which we are able to distinguish a something from nothing at all. The problem of distinguishing a something from nothing—if it is truly a problem—comes up in theological circles with regard to certain remarks ascribed to mystics. If God is truly Nothing, as the mystics sometimes suggest,[68] how is he to be distinguished from nothing at all? Surely there is some distinguishing characteristic, some characteristic which he possesses and which nothing does not possess. If there is, of course, then God is not after all Nothing. Put generally, what minimal characteristic would anything have to possess for it to be a something and not nothing? The answer to this question has usually been: just some characteristic or other.

Now if something has a particular characteristic, it is in some manner determinate. This is obvious in the case of families of mutually incompatible characteristics such as, for instance, those indicated by the conceptual framework of color terms. If an object is red, it is in that same respect neither blue, nor green, nor yellow, and so on. With respect to a certain domain of predicates the object is determined. Having one of these predicates applicable to it excludes it from embracing the others. Further, it has gained a distinguishing characteristic by which it is marked off from a large number of other objects to which the given predicate is *not* applicable. A partial identification of the object can be effected by means of this characteristic. In short, the object is in one respect at least *determinate*.

The same holds for characteristics which do not sustain to each other the relation of mutual incompatibility or exclusion. If any given predicate applies to an object, then the negation of that

68. See in this connection Evelyn Underhill, *Mysticism* (New York, 1958).

predicate does not so apply. Here again the object has become in a certain respect determinate.

If a something avoids being nothing by virtue of having at least one determinate characteristic, then whatever it is that enables that something to have such a determinate characteristic is the source of that something's Being, the source of that which distinguishes that something from nothing at all. Put in a formal mode of speech, this source is the pure form of connection which holds together yet articulates the various structural ingredients of statements in their formal constitution. Less formally, Heidegger holds that this source is Being itself; that happening, not itself an entity, is in some way akin to something living, emerging, and enduring, which happens only with respect to entities, and with respect to every entity. In short, Being is the source of and the actual Being of beings. In the midst of this the revisionary tendencies of Heidegger's philosophy must be remembered. To discover the pure form of connection together with its variants as it resides in Western languages is to acquaint oneself with a not altogether perspicuous picture which has held Western philosophers captive.[69]

In the last paragraph I used the phrase 'Being of beings'—an important phrase which requires a brief explanation. What constitutes a something *as* a something in Heidegger's view is its having at least one determinate characteristic, though this represents a limiting case. Another way of phrasing this point is to say that somethings as somethings are constituted by their *being* such and such. Heidegger relies chiefly upon this participial construction, choosing to refer to somethings as beings *(Seiende)*. This has two advantages. First, it preserves the notion of determinate characteristics as determinative of somethings as somethings. Second, it exhibits the intimate connection which somethings have with Being. Being *(Sein)* gives to beings *(Seiende)* their "is" *(ist)*, their being *(seiend)* such and such, and thus their Being *(Sein)*. Being, in other words, confers upon beings their determinateness,

69. Heidegger, *Identität und Differenz* (Pfullingen, 1957), g.72–73, e.66. The English edition I refer to is the Leidecker translation. See *Essays in Metaphysics,* trans. Kurt Leidecker (New York, 1960). Hereafter cited as ID.

which is their Being. As can be seen from this, there is thus (and perhaps only) a pedagogical reason for capitalizing 'Being' in English commentaries and translations, namely, so as to be able to refer to *Seiende* as beings, thereby preserving the close connection with *Sein* (Being), with a minimum of confusion and ambiguity of reference.

The connection with ordinary language is slightly tenuous here, for in English at least the participle 'being' seldom if ever functions in such ways as to tempt one to the construction of the notion of beings as a terminus technicus. If it does so function, it clearly does not do so elegantly. Most commonly participles are used as parts of a verb phrase.

> I am *asking* (present active participle)
> I have *asked* (past active participle)
> I am *being asked* (present passive participle)
> I have *been asked* (past passive participle)

Here the term 'being' functions as an element in the present passive participial construction, but it does not, so to speak, stand by itself. Rather, it requires a transitive verb put in past tense form to complete its meaning. The particular type of word the present passive participial construction requires is important to note. Granting that Being is a happening that happens to beings, it would not make much grammatical sense—or philosophical sense either—to say, for instance, 'the tree is being Beinged (or happened)' on the model of 'the wine is being aged.' 'To happen' *(geschehen)* is not a transitive verb and does not take an object. It is therefore not substitutable into present passive participial constructions. What follows from this grammatical point philosophically, of course, is that Being cannot be viewed as an agent that *does* something to entities. It would make slightly more sense to say 'the tree is being happened to' or, more grammatically, 'something is happening to the tree,' thereby preserving the dative as opposed to accusative commitment of the verb 'happen.' Thus one might say something like this: only insofar as an entity is being happened to does it have Being and can it be referred to as a being. Its being happened to is what constitutes its Being and makes it a being. But this would be a very odd way of talking.

Note finally that the present passive participial construction handles situations which have their locus in a *continuous* present. If the Being of entities is somehow or other constituted by their being happened to, then for them to have Being presupposes certain features to be characteristic of time. Put in a relatively simple way this is the force of the title *Being and Time* and the burden of its philosophical argument.

Clearly it makes no grammatical sense to use 'being' in isolation in a present active construction: 'I am being' standing by itself is at best a source of humor for philosophers. There are however some peculiarities about the present active construction. Whereas 'I am being obnoxious' is a perfectly grammatical though perhaps unusual remark to make, 'I am being tired' betrays its speaker as not being altogether familiar with the language. Some adjectival phrases are suited for incorporation into contexts involving the continuous present, some are not; and the use of 'being' in present active participial construction involves, as does its passive counterpart, this same notion of a continuous present. It turns out to be the case in Heidegger's view that the features which characterize the Being of an entity are in every instance to be understood in terms of such a continuous present.[70] However, this can represent only a necessary and not a sufficient condition for identifying a characteristic of an entity as a characteristic of that entity's Being —in short, for identifying it as an *ontological* characteristic. There are *ontic* characteristics which satisfy this same criterion. ('Ontic' is a term Heidegger makes much use of in *Being and Time*.[71] It is roughly equivalent to '*non*ontological' and refers thus to characteristics of an entity which are not characteristics of that entity's Being.)

If an entity has Being, we must at least be able to say of it some true statements of the form 'it is being such and such.' To ascribe Being to an entity is at least to place that entity in a continuous present. Characteristics of Being are only possible in such a time segment. For Heidegger, in fact, the Being of an entity first gives that entity a status whereby true statements of the form 'it is being

70. SZ g.25–26, e.47–49; g.17 ff., e.38 ff.; g.323 ff., e.370 ff.
71. SZ g.11–15, e.31–35.

x' can be made concerning it—regardless, even, of whether the *'x'* is an ontic or an ontological term.[72] Thus in Heidegger's view *Being* gives to *beings* their *Being;* and only as a result of this can it be said of them, among other things, that they are *being x.* This too is odd, and it carries us far beyond grammatical considerations. The connection of the terminus technicus 'being' with ordinary language in both this case and the case of the present passive participle depends clearly on extragrammatical factors and is thus, linguistically speaking, contrived. This is not to say, however, that this view is incoherent.

Other grammatical facts about participles need not detain us long. After their role as parts of verb phrases, the next most common use of participles is as adjectives. They can modify nouns and pronouns, can take objects in much the same manner as verbs do, and can themselves be modified by adverbs. For instance,

> a *coming* era
> *following* the clues, he found the chest
> the car, *rolling* crazily

It makes no sense at all to refer to a *being x,* understanding *x* to be something referred to by a noun or pronoun. According to Heidegger, the Being of something is no ordinary property of that something[73]—a fact which perhaps is grammatically indicated by this and by the further fact that 'a Being *x*' is equally without sense. Since 'to be' is an intransitive verb, 'being' cannot, like 'following' in our second example, take an object. The third example presents us with a slightly more intriguing issue. Granting that Being is a happening, what adverbial modifiers does it make sense to apply to the term 'Being?' More radically, is the term susceptible of any adverbial modification whatsoever? Heidegger's answer to the latter question appears to be affirmative. Throughout *Being and Time,* Heidegger coins very peculiar adverbial terms and phrases, whose significance is difficult to assess.

Let me return for a moment to the second example. Though the term 'being' cannot take an object, there are numerous instances

72. SZ g.10–11, e.30–31.
73. SZ g.38–39, e.63.

in everyday speech of the employment of this term at the beginning
of a dependent clause. Take, for instance, the following statement:

Being very tired, he went to bed early.

Though 'being' does not take an object, it qualifies the subject of
the sentence and determines that subject in a definite way. Again
the continuous present is involved in this determination. The sentence thus illustrates the two basic factors which constitute the
participial genesis of Heidegger's question of Being: the notion of
being as involving determination, and a commitment to a certain
continuous view of time. I should remark here that from a grammatical and formal standpoint, 'Since he was very tired, he went
to bed early' is more elegant; nonetheless, in everyday speech the
participial construction is prevalent.

Participles also enter into absolute constructions—constructions
in which the participle is used in a phrase relating to the whole
sentence (to the situation), rather than to a particular word. For
example,

'Judging from her looks, she isn't over twenty.'

It is difficult to know what to say here. No use of 'Being' appears to
be incorporable into such contexts. It might be surmised that this
parallels grammatically Heidegger's insistence that Being is always
the Being of an entity. The difficulty with this interpretation,
however, occurs when we try to determine the number of domains
over which Heidegger intends the term 'entity' (Seiend) to range.
Through simple transformations, absolute constructions can be
changed into statements embodying adjectival participial clauses
which modify a term standing for the entire situation which was the
subject matter of the absolute construction; but such transformations are somewhat contrived. This circumstance may save the
grammatical parallel to the point about Being in relation to entities by suggesting the stipulation of a certain limit to the domain
of denotation for the term 'entity' (Seiend). By way of example,

Judging from her looks, she isn't over twenty.

might be transformed (with no claim whatsoever of equivalence)
into,

Being hasty, his judging from her looks that she was under twenty-one was suspect.

Here 'Being' modifies 'judging,' a term indicating an act, but in a larger sense it modifies the entire clause and thus has reference not to an entity narrowly conceived, but to a whole situation. But these are perhaps questions for transformational grammarians.

One final point about the participle 'being': Heidegger often thinks of it as a metalinguistic device.[74] Accordingly he employs it to refer to 'is,' 'am,' 'are,' and related terms as they occur in object languages. Thus if we say

'the ball is red'

to speak of its "*being* red" is at least in part to comment on the 'is' in this sentence. The concern with the participial dimension of the verb 'to be' ties back in at this point with the most straightforward ordinary uses of the verb. And it is this straightforward use—itself ultimately to be understood in a revisionary manner—that provides the locus for most of Heidegger's linguistic excursions. He writes:

> The difficulty is one of language. Our western languages are languages variously suited to metaphysical thinking. Whether the nature of western languages bears only the stamp of metaphysics . . . or whether these languages offer other possibilities of expressing and at the same time saying without expressing, must remain an open question. During the exercises in our seminar often enough difficulties arose to which verbal expression of thought was exposed. The little word 'is' which is met everywhere in our language and tells of Being even where it does not come to the fore, harbors the entire fate of Being, from the ἐστιν γαρ ειναι of Parmenides to the 'is' of the speculative principle of Hegel and still further to the dissolution of the 'is' in the positing of a will to power by Nietzsche.[75]

Before drawing some conclusions to our preliminary discussion of the term 'Being,' two further points should be mentioned. Ac-

74. EIM g.68–70, e.76–77.
75. ID g.72 e.66.

cording to Heidegger, Being and beings are not comparable.[76] It is in effect a category mistake to try to compare them. The Being of a house, an *ontological* character of that entity, is not like the color of the house, an *ontic* property. Heidegger holds that past philosophers have nonetheless usually understood Being—if they have concerned themselves with it at all—to be an entity, usually the highest or supreme entity. Alternatively, he thinks, it has been viewed as a superproperty.[77] In either case, Heidegger holds that the logical behavior of 'Being' and its modifiers has been assumed to be similar to the logical behavior of terms referring to entities and their characteristics. In contrast with this traditional interpretation, Heidegger ascribes to ontological terms a different logico-conceptual disposition than that applicable to the ontic domain. Much of the purpose, in fact, of *Being and Time* as initially conceived was to exhibit, clarify, and articulate this disposition. Thus, to ask for the meaning of Being is to involve oneself in logical and conceptual issues from the start. Here, however, grave difficulties arise. Clearly these issues are further complicated by the absence of proper terms and grammatical devices with which to exhibit the conceptual properties possessed by Being. The paucity of metalinguistic terms and grammatical devices for dealing with the conceptual interrelations of the constituent elements of "happenings" is, I think, obvious, especially when one considers that the locus of such happenings is the conceptually puzzling continuous present. Heidegger himself alludes to these difficulties very early in *Being and Time*.

> With regard to the awkwardness and "inelegance" of expression in the analyses to come, we may remark that it is one thing to give a report in which we tell about *entities,* but another to grasp entities in their *Being.* For the latter task we lack not only most of the words but, above all, the "grammar." If we may allude to some earlier researches on the analysis of Being, incomparable on their own level, we may compare the ontological sections of Plato's *Parmenides* or the fourth chapter of the seventh book of Aristotle's *Metaphysics* with a

76. SZ g.38–39, e.63.
77. SZ g.3, e.22–23.

narrative section from Thucydides; we can then see the altogether unprecedented character of those formulations which were imposed upon the Greeks by their philosophers. And where our powers are essentially weaker, and where moreover the area of Being to be disclosed is ontologically far more difficult than that which was presented to the Greeks, the harshness of our expression will be enhanced, and so will the minuteness of detail with which our concepts are formed.[78]

Etymology and ordinary usage are to provide clues in the search for the meaning of Being, but conceptual interpretation of these clues is another matter. It is at this point that all of the repellent linguistic and grammatical peculiarities of "Heideggerese" first manifest themselves. And this is to say that in important respects oddities in Heidegger's expression are fundamentally metalinguistic in origin. Whether these oddities can be eliminated, and whether and in what senses it is philosophically worthwhile to do so, are questions which remain to be considered. How one answers them depends on one's assessment of the conceptual credibility of the question of Being.

The last point concerns the Kantian orientation of Heidegger's discussion of Being. In Heidegger's view, when we experience anything at all, we experience and have some understanding of the Being of that something.[79] Further, *a necessary condition for the experiencing of any entity* is an experiencing and understanding of that entity's Being.[80] Being is thus, at least in the Kantian sense, *transcendental.* Since this perplexing transcendentality will concern us at greater length in each of the remaining chapters, I just mention it here as a factor to be kept in mind.

In this chapter my approach to the question of Being has been primarily, though not exclusively, linguistic. Phenomenologists— Heideggerians in particular—may object that this approach misses the mark. Being, these philosophers claim, is extralinguistic, and a

78. SZ g.38–39, e.63. I shall have more to say about specific grammatical and terminological difficulties as this study progresses.

79. SZ g.5, e.25.

80. SZ g.35, e.59; g.38, e.62; g.5, e.25.

concern with the extralinguistic, whether in the form of Heidegger's Being, Merleau-Ponty's unreflected perception, or Husserl's noematic correlates, is precisely what distinguishes Continental from analytic philosophy. This objection is a particularly important one. From the Continental side of philosophy it serves in its generalized form as one of the chief obstacles to rapprochement. The extralinguistic thrust of phenomenology, it is argued, shows analytic philosophy to be myopic with respect to its field of philosophical interest and excludes analytic philosophy from participation in phenomenological concerns. This objection is not convincing, however. In fact, as an objection to the first chapter of this study, it can be disposed of with great dispatch. If every entity has Being, then surely linguistic entities have Being too, particularly if, as Heidegger claims, language is the "House of Being." In short, the Heideggerian conception of Being requires that the various features of Being be reflected in the structures and characteristics of language. Though the "problem of Being" need not be solely linguistic, it must at least be this.[81]

Considered linguistically, the most obvious sense in which there is a problem concerning Being results from taking seriously the equivocal meaning of 'is' and its brothers 'am' and 'are.' If 'is' has a number of meanings, and these meanings are not reducible to the distinction between identity and predication, the term 'is' requires further analysis. To this extent, then, Being presents a problem, though to call this problem the problem of Being is a bit pretentious perhaps and in any case misleading. On the other hand, the sorting out, categorizing, and interrelating of the various meanings of 'is,' 'am,' and 'are'—not to mention their tensed variants—presents no mean problem for philosophy. If this work is done with care, I suspect that at the very least it will shed new light on some old problems in metaphysics and theory of knowledge. The problems I have in mind concern the nature of abstract entities, the criteria to be employed in establishing personal identity over time, referential opacity, and standard instances of

81. On the other hand, appeals to linguistic usage are seldom "merely" linguistic. Correctness of usage depends upon such extralinguistic factors as the situation and circumstances in which the words are used.

perceptual error. Undoubtedly other problems will be illuminated
also.

There is another more important sense, however, in which
Being can and should be discussed as a linguistic problem. Having
alluded to the problem before, I shall return to it here through an
extended quotation from Waismann.

> Reality is undivided. What we have in mind [when we say
> that the world is a cluster of facts] is perhaps that *language*
> contains units, *viz.*, sentences. In describing reality, by using
> sentences, we draw, as it were, lines through it, limit a part
> and call what corresponds with such a sentence a fact. In other
> words, language is the knife with which we cut out facts.
> (This account is oversimplified as it doesn't take notice of
> *false* statements.)

> Reality then is not made up of facts in the sense in which a
> plant is made up of cells, a house of bricks, a stone of mole-
> cules; rather, if you want a simile, a fact is present, in much
> the same sense in which a character manifests itself in a face.
> Not that I invent the character and read it into the face; no,
> the character is somehow written on the face but no one
> would on that account say that a face is "made up" of features
> symbolic of such-and-such traits. Just as we have to interpret
> a face, so we have to interpret reality. The elements of such
> an interpretation, without our being aware of it, are already
> present in language—for instance, in such moulds as the
> notion of thinghood, of causality, of number, or again in the
> way we render colour, etc.

> Noticing a fact may be likened to seeing a face in a cloud,
> or a figure in an arrangement of dots, or suddenly becoming
> aware of the solution of a picture puzzle: one views a com-
> plex of elements as one reads a sort of unity into it, etc. Lan-
> guage supplies us with a means of comprehending and cate-
> gorizing; and different languages categorize differently.

> "But surely noticing a face in a cloud is not inventing it?"
> Certainly not; only you might not have noticed it unless you

had already had the experience of human faces somewhere else. Does this not throw a light on what constitutes the noticing of facts? I would not dream for a moment of saying that I *invent* them; I might, however, be unable to perceive them if I had not certain moulds of comprehension ready at hand. These forms I borrow from language. Language, then, *contributes to the formation and participates in the constitution* of a fact; which of course, does not mean that it *produces* the fact.[82]

Consider Waismann's two major claims:

> Through the use of sentences "reality" gets interpreted—that is to say, it gets articulated into determinate elements (facts). Different languages, because of their differing sentential structures, perform this interpretive function differently.

The first claim can be put in a stronger or a weaker form. In its strong form the claim is that language actually does the articulating. The weaker thesis is that language reflects the articulation. The stronger claim entails the weaker, but not conversely. Assume first the stronger claim. If one adds to it acceptance of the formula "to be is to be determinate," language has a great deal to do with the determination of "what is." For something to be determinate is for it to have some characteristic or other, and it is by means of language that "reality" (to use Waismann's term) gets characterized. Through the use of language, characteristics emerge which demarcate and delimit entities.

Waismann claims that the molds of comprehension which enable language to function in this determinative way are already at hand within the structures of language itself. These molds, in short, are transcendental—a view which, it seems to me, is essentially correct. Through these molds explicit determination (characterization) first becomes possible. To use Heideggerian language, it is through them that entities first emerge thematically *as* entities and are allowed to be the entities that they are. It is in this sense

82. Antony Flew, ed., *Logic and Language*, 1st and 2d ser. (Garden City, 1965), p.148.

that Heidegger is correct in saying that language is the House of Being.

What is a *characteristic* of something? Of what is it a characteristic? How is it a characteristic of that something? More broadly conceived, how do we relate to "reality" and in what ways do we take it seriously? Answers to these transcendental questions are to be found through an examination of various structures embedded in our language. If Being is that which makes possible somethings with determinate characteristics, then an analysis of these linguistic structures ought to yield knowledge of Being. To speak of Being, I have suggested, is to speak of something closely related to a pure form of connection, together with its modes, which holds together yet articulates the various structural ingredients of statements in their formal constitution. I now suggest as another dimension of the problem of Being, linguistically conceived, the illumination within a given language of that which is akin to such a pure form and its modes. Such illumination, it seems to me, reveals what predisposes a language to characterize in the way it does, to pick out the entities it does in the ways it does. In short, such illumination reveals Being.

One need not assume the stronger form of Waismann's claim in order to establish this second linguistic dimension of the problem of Being. Assume the weaker thesis, that language *reflects* the articulation. Accept again the view that to be is to be determinate. For something to be determinate is for it to have some characteristic or other. Language reflects the ways in which "reality" is characterized. If Being is that which enables there to be somethings with determinate characteristics, an analysis of the structures embedded in language ought to yield knowledge of Being.

Waismann also claims that different languages, because of their differing sentential structures, perform the interpretive function differently. *If true,* this claim not only makes the problem of Being unavoidably linguistic, it makes it language-relative as well—one that cannot be dealt with apart from consideration of the predispositions of the particular language in which or in terms of which the problem is discussed. On this, however, more later.

I must conclude on a cautionary note. Though I have stressed two linguistic dimensions of the problem of Being, analysis of the 'is' and analysis of the linguistic structures by means of which characterization is achieved (or reflected), there is more to the problem than the linguistic considerations I have adduced in this chapter fully reveal. To locate and at least partially define a problem linguistically—however important this task may be—is by no means to "reduce" the problem to a matter of "mere" language. However, the philosophical force of this last statement is difficult to assess. It depends to a great extent upon how one understands language and, thus, by implication, the extralinguistic. This understanding, in turn, depends to an even greater extent upon one's understanding of meaning. It is to this that I now turn.

CHAPTER 2

The Meaning of Being

One of the central topics of concern for contemporary philosophers, whether analysts or phenomenologists, has been the concept of meaning. Members of both groups have claimed that the domain of meaning(s) is the exclusive preserve and only battleground of philosophy. Concerning the basic features of this domain, its limits and locus, however, there has been much controversy. In this chapter I wish to enter the controversy on the side of the phenomenological tradition and to present what might be termed the phenomenological position regarding meaning. This position, as I define it, is not coextensive with Heidegger's views on meaning, but it is suggested by and closely related to them. Thus I begin my work in this chapter with a critical analysis of the concept of meaning found in Heidegger's philosophy. Since Being for Heidegger *is* meaning, this discussion is continuous with the considerations of the first chapter. To bring the phenomenological position into focus I then compare it in its philosophical genesis with the development of analytic philosophy's understanding of meaning. Here I turn from a critical analysis of Heidegger's views to a brief discussion of the recent history of the concept of meaning. In the light of this discussion I reflect back upon the problem of Being which, as I have indicated, is in fact a set of problems concerning meaning and then conclude the chapter with the reformulation of the first of my guiding questions: What is meaning?

Heidegger's remarks about meaning are so peculiar that one wonders whether the topic is worth pursuing through the tortuous labyrinth of his prose. It is surely odd that he states the central question of his philosophy by asking the meaning of *Being* rather than the meaning of 'Being.' Here obviously there is a problem. It is generally agreed that words have meanings. It is not altogether as clear, however, that the items referred to by these words have meanings. To make such a claim, one might argue, may well be to succumb to an uncritical and illicit employment of the material mode of speech.

Let us first consider Heidegger's case in the broad context of phenomenology. In ordinary language the term 'meaning' and its variants often do function in a way which supports Heidegger's phenomenological phrasing of his question. Consider the following examples, which clearly represent the sorts of ordinary language contexts out of which the term 'meaning' arises in phenomenology as a terminus technicus:

> She means everything to me.
> For those with no background in industrial psychology, his
>   decisions have very little meaning.
> What do you take their presence to mean?
> I found the Klee exhibition quite meaningful.
> The sacraments mean nothing to some churchgoers.
> Just having the opportunity means a great deal to him.
> A red light means that you must stop.
> Nature is much more meaningful to some than to others.

Meaning is here ascribed to such disparate items as persons, acts, paintings, religious rites, objects produced by modern technology, nature, and abstract entities. Though commonplace, these statements raise some difficulties for ordinary language philosophy which suggest reasons for adopting the phenomenological point of view. Ordinary language philosophers often assert that meaning has its exclusive residence in language, that meaning is a property of words or complexes of words, and that meaning is to be understood in terms of the roles various words play.

To be sure, this ordinary language doctrine has plausibility in certain areas. Consider, for instance, its handling of possibilities. Though not altogether unproblematic, it makes sense to claim that the statement

> There is a possible fight going on over there.

is really a poor way of saying

> It is possible there is a fight going on over there.

The concept of the possible applies thus to the statement. It is a metalinguistic concept with epistemic import, not an indicator of an invisible region of the world, the region of "possible" entities.

This epistemic and basically metalinguistic way of handling the concept of possibility is not without its problems but these are not my concern. I wish to indicate that this strategy fails when applied to the concept of meaning. If meaning is a property solely of language, the concept of meaning ought to be a metalinguistic concept. Rather than applying to objects in the world, it ought to apply only to the language used in talking about these objects. If this is the case, the statements I have just offered which embody the concept of meaning are ill formed and terribly misleading. More particularly, the statements must be capable of being translated, as the possibility statement was, into what Carnap and others refer to as a formal mode of speech. A translation of any of these statements into a formal mode of speech, however, presents nearly insuperable difficulties. What these translations must produce are statements in which the term 'meaning' is no longer predicated of, or ascribed by indirection to, the various entities mentioned in the original statements. The term 'meaning' must in effect drop out of the straightforward statement made in the object language and reappear, if it is to appear at all, as a metalinguistic notion embodied in a metalinguistic statement that serves as a commentary on the (now modified) object language statement. Quite clearly this is a formula which licenses the abuse of ordinary language remarks.

I shall not pursue this point at the moment, however, for Heidegger's position is not what one might expect—even granting the ordinary language genesis of 'meaning' as a technical term in his phenomenological philosophy. Heidegger writes:

> When entities . . . have come to be understood . . . we say that
> they have *meaning* [*Sinn*] . . . Meaning is . . . not a property
> attaching to entities, lying "behind" them, or floating some-
> where as an "intermediate domain." . . . *only Dasein can be
> meaningful* [*sinnvoll*] *or meaningless* [*sinnlos*] . . . . all en-
> tities whose kind of Being is of a character other than *Dasein's*

must be conceived as *unmeaning* [*unsinniges*], essentially devoid of any meaning at all.[1]

If we take these statements seriously, it follows that strictly speaking the term 'meaning' is not applicable to entities other than Dasein—understanding 'Dasein' for the present as a term roughly synonymous with the term 'man.' In short, only Dasein has meaning. Yet Heidegger also writes:

> And if we are inquiring about the meaning of Being, our investigation does not then become a "deep" one [*tiefsinnig*], nor does it puzzle out what stands behind Being. *It asks about Being itself insofar as Being enters into the intelligibility* [*Verständlichkeit*—an alternative translation might be 'understandability'] *of Dasein.*[2]

and:

> In *Being and Time* the question of the meaning of Being is raised and developed *as a question* for the first time. . . . It is also stated and explained in detail what is meant by meaning, namely the disclosure of Being.[3]

In these passages resides the greatest single difficulty in Heidegger's philosophy, a difficulty which is the cause of many of the other problems which his work faces. It is surely remarkable that this pivotal inconsistency has not been dwelt upon in greater detail by Heidegger's commentators.

Consider first the statement

> [our investigation into the meaning of Being] asks about Being itself insofar as Being enters into the intelligibility of Dasein.

On this account what distinguishes the *meaning* of Being from Being *simpliciter* is that the *meaning* of Being is Being itself,

1. SZ g.151–52, e.192–93.
2. SZ g.152, e.193. Italics mine.
3. EIM g.64, e.70.

though only to the extent that Being has been revealed or brought
to light. In short, the meaning of Being is Being insofar as Being
has been understood. The distinction between Being and its meaning as described here is roughly parallel to the medieval distinction
between the formal and objective modes of an entity's Being—
between, for instance, the moon as it is in itself and the moon as
known.[4]

But now consider the phrase

> . . . what is meant by meaning, namely the disclosure of
> Being . . .

'Disclosure' is a member of a particularly dangerous family of slip-
pery words in philosophy. Let me call these words ing/ed words.[5]
Beyond providing a convenient piece of shorthand for purposes of
discussion, this nomenclature also names the difficulty. The *Oxford
Universal Dictionary* gives two meanings for the term 'disclosure.'
It can either mean

> the action of disclosing, opening up to view, or revealing;
> discovery, exposure (*ing* sense)

or

> that which is disclosed. (*ed* sense)

If 'disclosure' is understood in the *ed* sense, then to refer to the
meaning of Being as the disclosure of Being is to refer to it as Being
itself as disclosed. This interpretation squares with the first statement which we have brought under consideration

4. I refer of course to this distinction as it was understood by the
medievals, hardheaded realists that they were, and not as it was subsequently
appropriated by Descartes. Descartes modified the doctrine in the service
of a representationalism which leads to the conceptual schizophrenia at the
basis of much nineteenth- and twentieth-century idealism. Whatever other
philosophical peculiarities belong to Heidegger, he is neither a representationalist nor, in any ordinary sense, an idealist.

5. 'Disclosure' translates *'Offenbarkeit.'* Clearly the potentiality for
ambiguity is not as great in the German as in the English. In German it
exists more in the philosophical interpretation of the concept of *Offenbarkeit* than in ordinary language meanings of the term.

[our investigation into the meaning of Being] asks about Being itself insofar as Being enters into the intelligibility of Dasein.

If, however, 'disclosure' is understood in the *ing* sense, matters are entirely different. To refer to the *meaning* of Being as the *disclosure* of Being is now to refer to it as the disclosing of Being. And disclosing is precisely the sort of thing done by human beings. The meaning of Being now becomes a property of one kind of entity, man, and not an aspect of Being itself. And this interpretation in turn squares with the following statements:

(a) *only Dasein can be meaningful or meaningless.*
(b) all entities whose kind of Being is of a character other than *Dasein's* must be conceived as *unmeaning,* essentially devoid of any meaning at all.

How are these last remarks to be reconciled with the *ed* interpretation of 'disclosure' and the first of the statements we have just considered? I do not believe that Heidegger considers this question explicitly, though an attempt at reconciliation can be pieced together from various remarks he makes. One is tempted to offer the following argument in Heidegger's behalf: Being, after all, is a happening. In some writings—particularly the later ones, though seldom if ever in *Being and Time*—Heidegger speaks as if Being discloses itself.[6] If we take the happening which is Being as a disclosing, the *ing* and *ed* interpretations coincide. Being itself is disclosed, but since Being is a disclosing, what is disclosed is precisely this disclosing. The meaning of Being is thus that disclosing which is Being's disclosing of itself, a disclosing which in turn is Being itself and, as a disclosing of itself as a disclosing, Being itself as disclosed. Given the axiom of reduction,[7] plus definitions of the terms involved, this argument may in fact be analytic on semantic grounds. Leaving this question aside, however, there is another

6. ID g.62 ff., e.57 ff.
7. See Willard Quine, *Set Theory and its Logic* (Cambridge, 1963), p. 250: "*axiom of reducibility: Every propositional function φ is coextensive with a predicative one.* That is, $(\exists\psi)\,(x)\,(\psi!x\equiv\phi x)$, $(\exists\psi)\,(x)\,(y)$ $(\psi!\,(x,y)\equiv\phi\,(x,y))\dots$"

consideration which recommends this interpretation: it is compatible with statement (a) above that

> only Dasein can be meaningful or meaningless,

a statement which on the surface at least appears to nullify the present attempt at reconciliation.

Heidegger's prose style, even in the midst of the most contorted of arguments, has a poetic undertone to it. This is a source at once of brilliant particular insights and of dubious reasoning. Nuance and metaphorical suggestion yield relief from conceptual tangles, but in an extended argument they lose their moorings, depending at this turn on one suggested meaning, at that turn on another. I mention this here because the compatibility of statement (a) with the present effort to bring the *ing* and *ed* interpretations together depends flatly on a metaphor. The metaphor is one of which Heidegger takes much advantage. Consider the term 'disclose.' 'Disclose' is an achievement verb which is used properly only when two conditions are met. First, something must in actual fact be disclosed. Second, that something must be disclosed *to* someone. In particular if, as a special case, x discloses x, there must be some y to which x discloses itself. This y may of course be identical with x itself, as in some forms of "self-knowledge." For x to have truly disclosed x to y requires that y on its side *receive* (as opposed to *fail to receive*) the disclosure. There is a form of speech, not altogether common today, which has among its expressions such phrases as

> filled with the knowledge of
> filled with delight
> filled with wonder.

In this language, to receive knowledge can under certain circumstances be viewed as tantamount to being filled with knowledge. And this is not always an innocent way of construing the situation. The metaphorical notion of the reception of knowledge as having something poured into one and being partially filled with that something has haunted epistemology and philosophy of mind during a number of periods in the philosophical past.

Consider now the term 'meaningful' *(sinnvoll)*. It is easy for Heidegger to construe this in a metaphorical way to mean "filled

with meaning." To say that Dasein is meaningful, then, is to say—
now unpacking the metaphor—that Dasein has received meaning.
In accordance with this line of reasoning, to say that Dasein alone
can be meaningful or meaningless is but to say the following: entities other than Dasein cannot, as a matter of conceptual fact, receive meaning. Because it is a conceptual truth that they cannot
be filled with meaning, it makes no sense to say of them that they
are empty of meaning. In short, the predicates 'meaningful' *(sinnvoll)* and 'meaningless' *(sinnlos)* do not apply to them. Heidegger
writes:

> If we adhere to . . . [this interpretation of the concept of
> meaning] then all entities whose kind of Being is of a charac-
> ter other than *Dasein's* must be conceived as *unmeaning* [*un-
> sinniges*], essentially devoid of any meaning at all. Here
> 'unmeaning' does not signify that we are saying anything about
> the value of such entities, but it gives expression to an onto-
> logical characteristic. *And only that which is unmeaning can
> be absurd* [*widersinnig*].[8]

This means of overcoming the disparate tendencies in Heidegger's interpretation of the concept of meaning is clearly the course
Heidegger himself takes, perhaps unwittingly, in his later writings.[9]
It provides a clue for understanding much of what is going on in
these writings, and it is what makes them at once both intriguing
and to no small degree irritating, perhaps even scandalous.[10] Unfortunately there are two major weaknesses in this attempt at reconciliation.[11]

Being is always the Being of an entity. But, to quote the passage
again,

8. SZ g.152, e.193.

9. Clearly this is a matter of interpretation. My interpretation, I believe,
is particularly cogent in the light of such works as, say, *Gelassenheit* (Pfullingen, 1959).

10. See in this connection James M. Robinson and John B. Cobb, Jr.,
eds., *The Later Heidegger and Theology* (New York, 1963).

11. To my knowledge Heidegger does not deal with the problem of
reconciliation in any explicit fashion. Thus I am offering an alternative on
his behalf and interpreting his later writings as giving indication of a
sympathy on his part for this alternative.

all entities whose kind of Being is of a character other than
Dasein's must be conceived as *unmeaning,* essentially devoid
of any meaning at all.

If meaning is a property of Being, and yet entities which possess a
kind of Being other than Dasein's have no meaning at all, then
either they have no Being—which the quotation denies—or only
Dasein's Being has meaning. If only Dasein's Being has meaning,
then the question of the meaning of Being is equivalent to the question of the meaning of Dasein's Being. In *Being and Time,* however, Heidegger claims that the question of the meaning of Being,
though best approached through a consideration of the meaning of
Dasein's Being, is not identical with the question of the meaning of
Dasein's Being.[12] And yet this latter question is the only one Heidegger is able to deal with in *Being and Time.* He answers it to his
satisfaction and the book then ends, abruptly and far short of its
projected goal.

If Being is the Being of an entity, and meaning is a property of
Being, it makes some sense to ascribe meaning to entities, albeit in
a roundabout and indirect way. This depends on taking "belonging
to" as a transitive relation. If one goes on to deny to entities other
than Dasein any meaning whatsoever, though one does not deny
them Being, it then becomes tempting to ascribe meaning only to
Dasein itself and not to Dasein's Being. Being is something all
entities possess. If meaning were a property of Being, why do
entities other than Dasein have no meaning?

Add to this the realization that of all entities only Dasein is
capable of receiving Being's disclosure—that other entities are, in a
manner of speaking, ontologically mute—and the ground is fully
laid for understanding meaning to be a characteristic solely of
Dasein. And this of course is the reason why entities other than
Dasein are viewed to be essentially devoid of meaning. 'Meaning'
takes on the metaphorical commitments of 'meaningful,' namely,
filled with meaning qua having received meaning by means of a
disclosure. Meaning now becomes the disclosing of Being in the
sense of Dasein's disclosing of Being. On this model the only meaning to be found belongs to Dasein or at best to Dasein's Being, not

12. SZ g.436–37, e.486–88.

to Being as such, and the attempt at finding the meaning of Being ends in failure. This, I think, is the unexpressed shortcoming which curtailed the argument of *Being and Time* before its completion.

There is another difficulty: understanding Being to be the disclosing of Being it becomes impossible to distinguish between Being and the meaning of Being. The two become simply one and the same—referred to by means of one expression on one occasion and by the other expression at a different point. Yet in *Being and Time* Heidegger clearly distinguishes between the Being of Dasein and the meaning of Dasein's Being. If the reconciliatory efforts in which I have engaged are truly to be successful, such a distinction should not remain. But it does, and with it remains the philosophically ambiguous doctrine of meaning. This doctrine constitutes the most seminal and suggestive ambiguity in Heidegger's thought.

Knowing neither the force of the term 'Dasein' nor that of 'Being,' it is difficult to determine the philosophical importance of the equivocal doctrine of meaning or the plausibility of either alternative. Here I shall trace out and reconstruct in part the *ed* interpretation of meaning—viewing meaning as Being itself insofar as Being is disclosed. Since in his later writings Heidegger clearly holds to the *ed* interpretation, this strategy will best represent the direction of Heidegger's thought. Beyond this and more important, however, the *ed* interpretation holds the most promise for the raising and solving of the problems I have set myself.

Strictly speaking, the meaning of Being for Heidegger is not Being itself insofar as it *has been* disclosed, but Being itself insofar as it *can be* disclosed. Heidegger writes:

> That which can be articulated in interpretation . . . is what we have called meaning. That which gets articulated as such . . . we call the totality-of-significations [*Bedeutungsganze*]. This can be dissolved or broken up into significations. Significations, as what has been articulated from that which can be articulated, always carry meaning [. . . *sind . . . sinnhaft*].[13]

Aside from the puzzling notions it suggests concerning language, this passage is perfectly straightforward. It parallels in a rough and ready way Hegel's distinction between certainty and truth in the

13. SZ g.161, e.204.

Phenomenology of Spirit.[14] For Hegel, reason is certain of that which it has in its grasp and whose content it is able to articulate. What is within reason's domain in this manner is referred to as certain in itself. To articulate that which is certain in this way is to bring it to its truth. Knowledge is obtained in the full-fledged sense only when certainty and truth become one and the same—in short, only when they coincide. (In contemporary thought the doing of conceptual geography parallels in spirit this conception of philosophical knowledge, minus, of course, most of the dialectic.) Similarly, for Heidegger one has knowledge of Being only insofar as its meaning—what can be articulated or explicitly revealed to be constitutive of it—coincides with the totality of its significations—what has actually been so articulated. Given an understanding of meaning (certainty) whereby meaning is not only limited to begin with, but limited even in the face of dialectical machinations, and given further a reinterpretation of what constitutes a proper "dialectical move" in philosophy, the essential differences between Hegel and Heidegger come to light. To say anything more about this topic, however, will be to risk illuminating the obscure by the more obscure. Let it suffice to say that the distinction between certainty and truth is itself just another variant of the more classical distinction between intentions and their fulfillments. Thus the problem of meaning and the problem of signification are both properly considered only within the context of an extended discussion of intentionality.

Meaning, then, as I extend and endorse Heidegger's view, is Being insofar as Being can be articulated with respect to its structural moments. To seek the meaning of Being is fully to articulate —to make totally explicit—what can be articulated as the content of Being. Thus the meaning of Being is that most peculiar (and as yet unexplained) happening, not itself an entity, in some way akin to something living, emerging, and enduring, that happens only with respect to entities and happens with respect to every entity, itself brought to light and revealed. To express this as a linguistic

14. Hegel, *Phänomenologie Des Geistes* (Hamburg, 1952), g.79 ff., e.149 ff.; g.175 ff., e.272 ff. (The English edition I refer to is the Baillie translation. See *The Phenomenology of Mind*, trans. J. B. Baillie [London, 1961].)

THE MEANING OF BEING

point, what is here revealed is something not unlike a pure form of connection, together with its syntactical variants, which holds together yet articulates the various structural ingredients of statements in their formal constitution. In accordance with this view, using Heidegger's language,

> the *concept of meaning* embraces the . . . framework of what necessarily belongs to that which an understanding interpretation articulates.[15]

The philosopher whose doctrines most pervade Heidegger's thought in *Being and Time* is neither Aristotle nor Hegel, nor even Husserl; it is Kant. This is true no less with respect to Heidegger's account of meaning than with respect to his account of Being—though generally speaking in Heidegger's hands Kantian points of view undergo subtle transformations. In *Being and Time* Heidegger understands meaning, quite correctly I believe, to serve a transcendental function of much the same sort as that served by Being. In fact, the former function is but an extrapolation of the commitment expressed in the latter. Entities can be experienced to be the entities which they are only because one already has some comprehension of the meaning of the Being of these entities. Since meaning is the meaning of Being, and Being is always the Being of some entity or other, I thus understand entities themselves to be meaningful. I conclude this by taking "belonging to" as a transitive relation. One understands entities in terms of the meaning of their Being, a comprehension of which—putting the point in Kant's language—serves as a necessary condition for the possibility of experiencing those entities. In characteristic Heideggerian language Heidegger himself writes:

> what makes the relation to . . . [entities] (ontic knowledge) possible is the precursory comprehension of the constitution of the Being of . . . [entities], namely, ontological knowledge.[16]

and

15. SZ g.151, e.193.
16. Heidegger, *Kant und Das Problem Der Metaphysik* (Frankfurt a.M., 1965), g.20, e.15. The English edition I refer to is the Churchill translation. See *Kant and the Problem of Metaphysics*, trans. J. S. Churchill (Bloomington, 1962). Hereafter cited as KB.

> meaning is the upon-which of a projection in terms of which
> something becomes intelligible as something;[17]

What can be articulated as the content of Being makes possible an
experience of entities which have Being. It is no less true that this
meaning is said by Heidegger to make Being itself possible. Such
a remark, though correct if properly understood, is open to the unfortunate interpretation that meaning is in some way *beyond* Being.
This interpretation is unnecessary and, in terms of Heidegger's other
remarks, implausible. The meaning of Being is to Being as the parts
of a watch and their functional connections are to that watch itself,
not as uncooked meat is to indigestion. About this matter nothing
more need be said other than to point out what amounts to an
analytic truth: the meaning of Being does make the understanding,
or comprehension, of Being possible.

I have stated that the question of the meaning of Being is a
question which concerns the meaning of meaning. If meaning is
Being disclosed, it follows that Being is meaning undisclosed. Thus
to disclose Being is to disclose meaning, to effect the transition of
meaning from that state in which it is vaguely or unthematically
understood to the state in which it is thematically grasped and articulated. What Heidegger is striving for throughout his pursuit of
the question of the meaning of Being, then, is a general doctrine of
meaning.

We must explore the concept of meaning further, however. What
should be one's concern when one asks the nature of meaning? To
focus this question more clearly let us reconsider the concept of
meaning as it is embodied in another set of ordinary language
statements.

> Their absence from the meeting had considerable meaning.
> He means a great deal to me.
> Nature is especially meaningful to people with rural back-
> grounds.
> I didn't find Albers' paintings as meaningful as I had anti-
> cipated.

17. SZ g.151, e.193.

To many of the faithful the sacraments mean little.

A yellow light means that one should exercise caution.

The number seventeen had many meanings (much significance) for him.

For those versed in social psychology, his maneuverings had a great deal of meaning.

In these statements, as in the previous set of statements, meaning is ascribed to a wide variety of disparate items. There is nothing particularly odd about these statements. They simply reflect the nature of human experience, the objects of which are found to be meaningful in a variety of different ways. From this circumstance follows my major point: if we commence our philosophizing about the concept of meaning with a consideration of the term 'meaning' and its variants as they are ordinarily used, clearly we are compelled to regard meaning as being as much, if not more, a feature of nonlinguistic entities as of linguistic entities. Any general doctrine of meaning must take this into account. Obvious as this requirement may seem, however, it is by no means uncontroversial. It raises considerable difficulties for ordinary language philosophy and analytic philosophy in general. For philosophers of these persuasions meaning is fundamentally, if not solely, a property of words or groups of words. Ryle catalogues the development of this position with great insight.[18] In doing so he shows that the position's alternative—that meaning is with equal justice to be ascribed to things (that is to say, to nonlinguistic entities)—has not been seriously considered.

The starting point of Ryle's historical résumé is Mill's theory of meaning. Ryle claims that there are in effect two ways of construing this theory, a "denotationist" way and a "connotationist" way. Let us consider the former first. According to Ryle, Mill follows Hobbes in taking the single word as the basic unit in the theory. As might be expected, the only entities which are allotted meaning are linguistic entities. The meaning of a sentence (or phrase) is viewed as a compound of the meanings of the single words that go into

18. See Gilbert Ryle, "The Theory of Meaning," in *Philosophy and Ordinary Language,* ed. Charles E. Caton (Urbana, 1963), pp. 128–53.

the makeup of the sentence (or phrase). Mill takes it for granted
that nearly all such single words are names. A name for him, however, is not what contemporary philosophers term a proper name.
According to Ryle, Mill holds two, slightly differing views on the
nature of a name: that a name is any expression which can fit into
the subject place in a subject-predicate sentence, and that a name is
any expression which can fit either into the subject or the predicate
place in a subject-predicate sentence. On either view the meaning
of a single word is the same. It is the thing of which the word is a
name. This is the essence of the denotationist position. Ordinary
objects, thus, among other things, are understood to be meanings.
As we shall see, the contrast with the phenomenological tradition
is striking. For Mill the denotationist the objects of experience do
not *have* meanings; rather, they *are* meanings. The only items that
have (or bear) meanings are names. This denotationist position,
presumably, is the starting point for the analytic tradition's reflections on the concept of meaning.

Ryle catalogues the major objections which the analytic tradition has raised against the denotationist account. In no way,
however, do these objections bring into question the view that
meaning is primarily, if not exclusively linguistic. It is assumed
all along that basically meaning is a property of language. The objections are four in number. In the first place, two phrases can have
the same referent but different meanings. The meaning of a single
word or phrase, thus, cannot be the referent of that word or phrase.
Here, of course, we encounter various problems presented by intentional contexts and the puzzles surrounding the phenomenon
of referential opacity. The classic example of referential opacity is
given by Frege, that of 'the morning star' and 'the evening star.'[19]
Clearly, though the two phrases 'the morning star' and 'the evening
star' have the same referent, the planet Venus, one phrase cannot
be substituted for the other in certain statements without falsifica-
tion of those statements. Though it is true, for instance, that

19. Other examples could, of course, be adduced. This one, however,
seems the simplest to deal with.

> the evening star was first identified with the morning star by the Babylonians,

it is not true that

> the morning star was first identified with the morning star by the Babylonians,

and it is not true that

> the evening star was first identified with the evening star by the Babylonians.

The phrases 'the morning star' and 'the evening star,' thus, are not synonymous in meaning. Since their referent is the same, their meaning cannot be their referent. Note one important feature of this sort of objection, however, a feature shared by the other objections yet to be presented. The argument assumes that words have meanings. It argues that things, nonlinguistic entities, cannot *be* those meanings. But the argument says nothing about whether nonlinguistic entities, though not themselves meanings, have meanings and, if they do, what status such meanings possess. Because the argument concerns itself exclusively with meaning as a property of words and the character of that sort of meaning, I shall term the argument *meaning monoscopic.* It is clear that the analytic tradition as a whole is in this sense meaning monoscopic.

The second objection attacks more directly Mill's putative theory concerning single words. If every word is a name, sentences are lists of the objects named by their component words. Such a list, however, is not a sentence, for it has no truth value, and sentences sometimes do have truth values. Lists of names cannot be true or false, but sentences more often than not *are* true or false. To have meaning, thus, is not the same as to stand for something. These notions are by no means coextensive. Note again the meaning monoscopic character of this objection, however. What is in question is not the geography of meaning as such, but only the nature of linguistic meaning.

A third objection is that descriptive phrases can be coined to which nothing corresponds, e.g. 'the golden mountain' and 'the angry centaur.' Though these phrases designate nothing, they do have meaning, a fact for which the denotationist aspects of Mill's theory does not allow. If there is nothing which a word denotes, on the denotationist view the word must be without meaning. But this is a philosophical doctrine that flies in the face of obvious linguistic facts. Not infrequently do we speak meaningfully of centaurs, unicorns, and even witches. Clearly these do not exist, however, and names for them, thus, have no bearers. Yet, notwithstanding the validity of this particular objection to denotationism, it, too, is meaning monoscopic. The objection is only concerned with the locus of linguistic meaning.

Finally, most words are not nouns. From a grammatical point of view a word that is not a noun cannot be a name. Now, as Ryle indicates, Mill himself holds that 'is' and other syncategorematic terms are not names. Mill's claim is that syncategorematic terms help in the construction of what contemporary philosophers term definite descriptions. Rather than naming extra things, syncategorematic terms are ancillary to the "multi-verbal" naming of things. Yet as is pointed out by the analytic tradition, terms such as 'is' certainly have meanings. With this admission the doctrine that only names have meanings collapses and with it the denotationist aspects of Mill's theory of meaning. But this final objection, too, is meaning monoscopic. It is concerned with meaning as a property of language, not as a property of things. The latter possibility is in no way considered.

We turn now to the connotationist strain in Mill. Ryle points out that for Mill most words and descriptive phrases perform two simultaneous functions: they denote their bearers and connote the characteristics by which their bearers are described. The objections to Mill's denotationist account of meaning are rendered in large measure irrelevant, it is presumed, by a simple fact. The meaning of a word for Mill, Ryle claims, is actually its connotation, though Mill did not state this doctrine explicitly and those who followed him emphasized for the most part his denotationist side. Mill says that proper names only denote. They do not *mean* anything. Proper names are arbitrary labellings and thus convey no truth or falsehood. In fact, they convey nothing at all.

At this point in his account Ryle interprets and endorses Mill's "connotationist" position in the light of contemporary analytic philosophy's doctrines concerning meaning. To consider the meaning —Mill's connotation—of an expression is to consider what can be said with it, truly or falsely, and the ways it can be used in acts of requesting, commending, advising, commanding and all other sorts of sayings. Ryle thinks of this—needless to say, monoscopically —as the normal sense of 'meaning.' In terms of this normal sense the meaning of a subexpression, a word or phrase, for example, is a function of the range of possible questions, commendations, assertions, and so on, into which the word or phrase can enter. A word's meaning, thus, is a function of what can be done with the word, its role within actual and possible sayings. Ryle calls it the "distinguishable common locus" of a range of possible tellings, advisings, questionings, etc. Here we have a functionalist view of meaning. As might be expected, it shares an important feature in common with the denotationist view. Like the denotationist position this functionalist, connotationist view of meaning is meaning monoscopic. It locates the meaning of words in their functional position within the linguistic matrix of a community of language users. It says nothing, however, about the status of nonlinguistic entities, whether they have meaning and, if so, what their meanings are. To emphasize even more strongly the meaning monoscopic character of the analytic tradition's views all one needs do is trace out Ryle's historical account of the fate of Mill's views on meaning.

Ryle claims that Mill's doctrine of denotation, minus its qualifications and safeguards, was taken up by Mill's successors, while his connotationist views were left behind. He offers two reasons for this selective appropriation of Mill's position. First, 'connote' has close affinities with the term 'imply,' which is not what is desired in a theory of meaning. The notion of implying is too subjective and variable in its own "connotation." Second, Mill himself soon contaminated his connotationist doctrine with a plethora of irrelevant and questionable material drawn from associationalist and sensationalist psychology. Influenced by these two factors, Mill's successors, believing that they were preserving what was valid in Mill's position, held that to mean was to denote. They also held that all significant expressions were proper names and that what proper names meant was what the names were names of; in short, the meaning of proper names was understood to be their bearers. This doctrine of linguistic meaning, understood to be a doctrine of meaning as such, became the center of considerable controversy, preoccupying the analytic tradition for some time.

As can be seen by cursory inspection, the denotationist position was fraught with difficulties. Committed to the view that the meaning of a term was its denotation and confronted with general nouns, the nominalistically inclined denotationists, Ryle states, were forced, it appeared, to accept Platonic entities into their universe. How else could one deal, for instance, with the meaningful term 'dog'? The precise denotation of adverbs and prepositions was never satisfactorily explained either. What did 'with' denote, or 'of,' or 'slowly'? The same general puzzles arose over denotations of various clauses and complexes of words having unitary meanings.

Still further problems arose over intentional inexistents. Whenever a sentence is constructed in which a grammatical subject and its verb can be distinguished, the grammatical subject must have a meaning if the sentence is to have a truth value. Put in another way, if the sentence has a truth value, the grammatical subject must have a meaning. On the denotationist view, however, the grammatical subject, if meaningful, must denote something which is there to be named. Granting this, it is hard not to conclude, as Meinong actually did, that surd entities such as round squares have some kind of reality. It is false that

a round square is on my typewriter case.

But if the sentence is false, it has a truth value. On the denotationist view the sentence's grammatical subject, 'a round square,' therefore, must denote something. This ontological commitment was obviously difficult for the denotationists to accept. Matters were complicated even further, however, for it was seen clearly that

round squares did not exist.

What then was their status? All the puzzles that arose over this question plagued the denotationist position. The meaning monoscopic view that linguistic meanings were the bearers of names and that these bearers were, among other things, the ordinary objects of experience became less and less tenable. However, as Ryle's chronicle shows, the preoccupation with meaning as linguistic meaning continued.

As Ryle indicates, more than anything else it was Russell's work that brought about the downfall of the denotationist position. Russell developed a doctrine of incomplete symbols. Incomplete symbols are expressions which have no meaning—that is to say, no denotation—by themselves. Their function, Russell claimed, was to be auxiliary to expressions which do denote. Ryle interprets Russell to be claiming in effect that descriptive phrases are just as syncategorematic as 'or,' 'not,' and 'are.' These latter phrases, of course, had already been accepted as syncategorematic in the work of Mill. As Ryle interprets him, Russell was virtually claiming that the meanings of many expressions are not to be found in what they name, but in how they are used. Improperly used, certain expressions become meaningless. Properly used those same expressions are meaningful. In Ryle's chronicle Russell's significant advance was to work out a distinction which Mill had grasped but not himself developed, the distinction between sentences which have truth value and sentences which, though syntactically correct and proper in vocabulary, are without meaning and therefore without truth value. What results is that meaning is seen to be the obverse of the nonsensical. The meaning of a term is detached from its bearer and attached to the term's function, the manner in which the term is capable of being used. In a context where a term is used improperly, that term becomes meaningless and the context itself, the sentence or phrase in which the term appears, loses its meaning. Here we see the beginnings of a major change in the analytic tradition's way of construing linguistic meaning. Note that this change leaves untouched the assumption that, for philosophical purposes at least, meaning is primarily, if not solely, linguistic.

What followed from Russell's work, Ryle claims, was that meaning came to be viewed as belonging to the domain of logic. Traditionally it was the logician's concern to determine rules for the correct employment of language. Because part of the logician's task was to establish and codify rules of this sort—that is, to determine validity—the notion of meaning came to be viewed as a set of rules for the proper (valid) employment of words and phrases. On this view knowledge of the meaning of an expression involved knowing the uses to which the expression could and could not be put—in short, knowledge of the rules in accordance with which the expression could properly (validly, meaningfully) be employed. The task of gathering this knowledge fell, presumably, to the logician.

There are some things worth noting about this development of the influential doctrine of logical atomism. They explain in part the dearth of empiricism in the mainstream of analytic philosophy earlier in this century. To begin with, logic is more an a priori than an empirical science. If meaning is the proper concern of logicians, the study of meaning begins to lose its empirical dimension. Further, to the degree to which the concern with meaning becomes "logical," one's understanding of meaning becomes even more monoscopic. What, after all, is more divorced from the objects of human experience in their richness of content and in the meanings they bear than logical considerations which are either formal or abstractly transcendental? Yet, and this point I wish to emphasize, given the analytic tradition's starting point—a set of puzzles surrounding the nature of linguistic meaning—this development into the realm of logic and away from the notion of nonlinguistic bearers of meaning was almost inevitable.

It was the Tractarian Wittgenstein, Ryle continues, who presented this new "logical" approach to meaning in its most concise and influential form—a form not unsullied, however, by denotationist elements. Wittgenstein held that sentences were not names. To say something, thus, was not necessarily to name something. One could speak meaningfully without having to name anything in the process. Logical constants did not represent; in fact, they denoted nothing whatsoever. They were syncategorematic expressions, not names. Along with Frege, Wittgenstein saw that the questions asked by logicians were not questions about the relations or properties possessed by the denotata, if any, of the expressions under investigation. Rather, they were questions concerning the logical behavior of those expressions. All linguistic elements capable of entering into sentences, Wittgenstein thought, were governed by certain rules, rules of "logical syntax" and "logical grammar." When words were combined in such a way that the result was nonsensical, it was these rules that were broken. Logic for Wittgenstein included and was perhaps identical with the study of these logico-syntactical or logico-grammatical rules. There in almost its pure form we find the "logical" approach to meaning.

As Ryle points out, early in the twentieth century Husserl too had worked with the notion of a "logical grammar." What Ryle does not point out, however, and what should be obvious from what has been said, is that, contrary to Husserl and the phenomenological tradition, the concern with meaning in Russell, the Tractarian Wittgenstein, and the logical atomists was solely linguistic. The only thing in question was the meaning of linguistic elements. The concern was meaning monoscopic.

To bring his brief historical résumé to a conclusion, Ryle turns to the work of the later Wittgenstein, undoubtedly the dominant influence on contemporary Anglo–American philosophy. Ryle indicates that the later Wittgenstein separated himself completely from the denotationist position. Remaining meaning monoscopic, Wittgenstein's advance, it seems to me, was precisely this separation. Ryle's account bears this out. For Wittgenstein, the meaning of an expression—and this is the only kind of meaning discussed, either by Ryle or by Wittgenstein—has great affinities with the function performed by a particular piece in a game of chess. Ryle claims that there are three major differences. First, whereas a person can be taught the rules of chess to a considerable extent before beginning to play, a person cannot be taught the rules of language in this way. Second, there are books of instruction for chess, but there are no similar manuals whose subject matter is meanings. Third, whereas rules for playing chess are definite and inflexible, linguistic rules are rather indefinite and for the most part highly flexible. To know what an expression means, then, is to know how to employ it and what modes of its employment would be improper —given of course the elasticity of the rules governing the expression's employment. Such is the later Wittgenstein's position. Coupled with this is the view that there is a large variety of types of uses which words accommodate. In short, words play many roles and there is a plethora of categories of meaning.

Meanings for Wittgenstein, Ryle continues, are not things, not even odd, mysterious things—a view which is perfectly compatible with the phenomenological view that things (nonlinguistic entities) have meanings. Learning a meaning, Wittgenstein holds, is learning to operate properly with an expression and its equivalents. The meanings of a term, thus, are the functions the term is able to perform in the various language games into which it enters. As might be expected, nothing is said concerning nonlinguistic meaning.

I have dealt at some length with Ryle's historical résumé because I think it is important to see in concrete terms the monoscopic character of the analytic tradition's concern with meaning. Ryle's account has the double advantage of being both concise and accurate. From it one sees that, in the analytic tradition, preoccupation with the difficult question of the nature of linguistic meaning has led to an implicit denial of meaning to nonlinguistic entities. Perhaps this denial is but a methodological one or simply the expression of a selective philosophical interest. Whatever the case may be, I believe that the denial has congealed into a dangerous dogma. It is one thing to say that the ordinary objects of experience are not the meanings of the terms we employ. It is quite another thing to conclude from this that nonlinguistic entities themselves have no meaning. These two theses are too often confused by analytic philosophers.

Part of the reason for the analytic tradition's stance can be found in its perennial concern, one might say preoccupation, with avoiding the philosophical commitments of Platonism. To explain how this is so, I revert again to Ryle's discussion. Ryle points out that in the seventeenth and eighteenth centuries, and for most of the nineteenth century, a philosopher was virtually any sort of savant. The term philosopher was applied to a chemist with as much justice as it was applied to Hume. For a considerable period of time there existed no word in English for those whom we now call scientists. The basic distinction was between natural philosophy on the one hand and moral and metaphysical philosophy on the other. The former included the physical and biological sciences, the latter almost everything else. Ryle claims that in England this distinction between the natural philosopher and the moral or metaphysical philosopher was understood to be a distinction between laboratory and introspective science. The natural philosopher studied external, physical phenomena by laboratory techniques. The moral or metaphysical philosopher—a kind of psychologist, a moral or mental scientist—studied internal mental phenomena by introspective methods. Ryle claims that three influences were primary in dispelling the view that doing philosophy was doing one or the other of the above. Though Ryle does not say so, all three influences, it is clear, led to conclusions which were highly accommodating to Platonic views. The first influence was the work of Frege, Husserl, and Russell to save mathematics and logic from the psychologizing analyses of Mill. Having exactness and universality, logical and mathematical truths, they thought, could not merely be empirical generalizations gained by induction and introspection. Thus, it was concluded, not all philosophy could be understood to be a mental science—granting logic to be a part of philosophy. There had to be a realm of "logical" objects, such items as implications, concepts, and so on. Clearly one could not help but view this domain as closely resembling a Platonic realm of ideas. Its independence from the realms of psychology and natural science made Platonic interpretations inevitable. The second influence was the development of experimental, laboratory psychology. If experimental or "scientific" psychology did actually absorb the problems arising out of a consideration of psychological states and processes, what was left for epistemologists, moral philosophers, and logicians to concern themselves with? Clearly the developments of experimental sciences of all sorts, particularly the science of experimental psychology, threatened the picture of the philosopher as an introspective savant. Given philosophers' concern to have a subject matter of their own, the threat posed by the sciences gave Platonism some encouragement. The third influence was broadly speaking phenomenological. Brentano, who simply follows Mill and the Medievals, maintained that mental processes and states were always *of* —that is so say, always directed toward—objects or contents. It was an a priori principle of psychology, Brentano thought, that consciousness was always consciousness of something. To explain this notion more clearly Ryle makes an insightful comparison with grammar. Grammatically speaking, a transitive verb requires for the completion of its meaning a term in the accusative case, a direct object. Parallel to this, acts of consciousness, it was thought, were themselves directed toward their own accusatives, their own direct or "intentional" objects. What was true of these acts of consciousness, often viewed as psychological states, was not necessarily true of their objects or contents, and vice versa. Ryle points out that Meinong and Husserl distinguished

> the various private momentary and repeatable acts of conceiving, remembering, judging, supposing and inferring from their public, non-momentary accusatives, namely, the concepts, and propositions and the implications which constituted their objective correlates.

Platonic conclusions were not hard to draw from this distinction. The view arose that there was a special realm, a realm populated with nonmaterial, nonmental items such as numbers, propositions, concepts, and classes.

All three influences worked together, it seems to me, to secure an autonomy for philosophy, separating it from the various sciences. The price of independence, however, appeared to be a commitment to some form of Platonism. This development was mostly unwanted, though its most significant result was not totally unexpected. The form the result took, however, deserves special attention. As Ryle indicates, Husserl and Meinong had construed the objects of acts of consciousness as belonging together. These objects were termed 'meanings' *(Bedeutungen).* Thus the inevitable attack on Platonism—and this point I wish to stress—became an attack on the view that there existed a separate realm of meanings. In short, to save philosophy from the influence of Platonism philosophers had to reinterpret the notion that meaning resided in a separate domain. But from what should the realm of meanings not be separated? The analytic tradition was concerned to determine the meaning of linguistic entities. Linguistic meaning, it was seen, could not be identified with natural objects. Besides the obvious difficulties involved in holding such a view, natural objects were believed to be the proper subject matter of science, not of philosophy. But to place meaning in between language and the objects it sometimes denoted, was to fall prey, it was thought, to Platonism. The only recourse left open was one hallowed by the respectable nominalist tradition. Linguistic meanings had to be located in language itself and in particular, in the various functions linguistic terms and phrases performed. To locate meaning anywhere else was either to commit oneself to Platonism or to fall prey to the incisive objections that had destroyed denotationism. To avoid Platonism, all meaning had to be located in the functional capabilities of linguistic elements.

The question to raise, of course, is whether the view that nonlinguistic entities have meanings is unavoidably Platonic. Does the claim that nonlinguistic entities are meaningful necessarily commit one to a third "free-floating" realm? I do not think that it does, and neither, it appears, do phenomenological philosophers such as Heidegger and Merleau-Ponty:

> When entities within-the-world are discovered along with the Being of Dasein—that is, when they have come to be understood—we say that they have *meaning* [*Sinn*]. But that which is understood, taken strictly, is not the meaning but the entity, or alternatively, Being.[20]

> The need to proceed by way of essences [meanings] does not mean that philosophy takes them as its object, but, on the contrary, that our existence is too tightly held in the world to be able to know itself as such at the moment of its involvement, and that it requires the field of ideality in order to become acquainted with and to prevail over its facticity. . . . Husserl's essences [meanings] are destined to bring back all the living relationships of experience, as the fisherman's net draws up from the depths of the ocean quivering fish and seaweed. Jean Wahl is therefore wrong in saying 'Husserl separates essences from existence.' [Merleau-Ponty documents this quotation as coming from *Réalisme, dialectique et mystère* (l'Arbalète), Autumn 1942.] The separated essences are those

20. SZ g.151, e.192–93.

of language. It is the office of language to cause essences to exist in a state of separation which is in fact merely apparent, since through language they still rest upon the ante-predicative life of consciousness. In the silence of primary consciousness can be seen appearing not only what words mean, but also what things mean: the core of primary meaning round which the acts of naming and expression take shape.

Seeking the essence of consciousness will therefore not consist in developing the *Wortbedeuting* of consciousness and escaping from existence into the universe of things said; it will consist in rediscovering my actual presence to myself, the fact of my consciousness which is in the last resort what the word and the concept of consciousness mean. Looking for the world's essence is not looking for what it is as an idea once it has been reduced to a theme of discourse; it is looking for what it is as a fact for us, before any thematization.[21]

Both quotations raise a number of difficult questions. They agree, however, in ascribing meaning in a nonseparatist way to nonlinguistic entities. The meanings of such entities, it is suggested, need not comprise a third realm—no more so, at least, than do the meanings of words. This suggestion is one I endorse. In working out the first of my guiding questions—what is meaning?—I wish to take the notion of nonseparatist, nonlinguistic meaning very much into account. But what sort of thing is the meaning of a nonlinguistic entity? What description of it is perspicuous while avoiding Platonic commitments? Up to this point I have done no more than to present two sets of ordinary language statements which exhibit states of affairs involving nonlinguistic meaning. What does one look for in seeking to demarcate conceptually meaning as an extralinguistically based phenomenon? I shall approach this question through another rather selective résumé, this time of the

21. Maurice Merleau-Ponty, *Phénoménologie de la perception* (Paris, 1945), f.ix–x, e.xiv–xv. The English edition I refer to is the Smith translation. See *Phenomenology of Perception,* trans. *Colen Smith* (New York, 1962).

phenomenological tradition and its struggle with the concept of meaning.[22]

Phenomenology grew out of the recognition of one very specific problem, which had haunted German philosophy since its beginnings in Leibniz.[23] There was, philosophers saw, no clearly defined, common method for doing philosophy. In the absence of such a method progress in philosophy, it was thought, was impossible. Philosophical controversy was merely a matching of opinion against opinion. No means were available for securing collaboration and agreement among investigators. In short, there existed no generally accepted, common method of adjudicating philosophical disputes and testing philosophical results. From the very beginning of phenomenological philosophy the emphasis was put on establishing a method of investigation that would correct this situation. This explains one of the central peculiarities of the phenomenological movement, the vagueness that surrounds phenomenology's conception of the object which it is to investigate. The phenomenologist's conception of the objects towards which his method is to be directed—I shall term these objects *meanings*—alters and, it seems, *only* alters, with the alteration of the method itself. The result, particularly in Husserl's work, is that more clarity exists concerning the nature of the method than concerning the objects upon which the method is practiced.[24]

The phenomenological method, it was thought, had to be free of metaphysical commitments.[25] It was to be "ontologically neutral" and without presuppositions. In fact, at its inception phenomenology was programmatically antimetaphysical. It understood meta-

22. Richard Schmitt has documented this struggle quite well in an article entitled "In Search of Phenomenology," *Review of Metaphysics 15* (March 1962): 450–79. Hereafter cited as IP.

23. IP 453. Though Schmitt does not trace the historical antecedents, it is clear that the researches of Leibniz, Kant, Fichte, and Hegel all grew in part out of the recognition of this problem.

24. In this connection see IP 458 ff.

25. This claim has given rise to a number of controversies and philosophical misunderstandings. For a discussion of some of the issues involved, see Marvin Farber, *The Aims of Phenomenology* (New York, 1966), pp. 18–42.

physics to be the discipline that went μετα τα φυσικα, beyond the physical. This it interpreted in accordance with Kant's views as the attempt to go beyond the experienceable. By taking an antimetaphysical stance, phenomenology first came to understand itself as a science of experience and then, under Husserl's guidance, as *the* science of experience.

This interpretation of phenomenology was reinforced by another requirement phenomenologists put upon themselves. Their method had to yield certain, as opposed to probable, truths.[26] They strove, therefore, to articulate a set of philosophical procedures which would secure an indisputable, intersubjectively verifiable body of knowledge. Here was another reason phenomenologists found for driving a wedge between the experienceable (their subject matter) and the nonexperienceable (the subject matter of metaphysics). Certain knowledge, it was thought, had to be knowledge which involved a direct encounter with what was to be known.[27] Phenomenologists thought their task was to *describe* such experienceable items, as opposed to explaining them.[28] Explanations, it was thought, often went beyond the realm of direct experience and involved a large number of assumptions. The objects of phenomenological investigation came to be viewed, thus, as anything directly experienceable insofar as it was capable of being described on the basis of that experience.

The manner in which certain knowledge was defined clarified the notion of the directly experienceable, and thus the notion of a meaning, a bit further. Not only did certain knowledge have to be assumption-free, doing no more than describing its object, it also came to be understood as knowledge of what was necessary for

26. Ibid., pp. 65 ff. See also IP 460 ff. The problem of "certainty" has never been treated with the systematic rigor it requires. To say the least, this circumstance is unfortunate.

27. Edmund Husserl, *Ideen Zu Einer Reinen Phänomenologie und Phänomenologischen Philosophie I* (Halle, 1928), g.43–44, e.92–93. The English edition I refer to is the Gibson translation. See *Ideas,* trans. Boyce Gibson (London, 1958). Hereafter cited as *Ideas.* See also IP 459 ff.

28. IP 462–63.

something to be what it was.[29] To have certain knowledge of a chair, for example, would be to have certain knowledge of those features or characteristics of the chair by virtue of which it was a chair rather than something else. It was thought that there was nothing else about the chair of which one could have certain knowledge. Given this understanding of certain knowledge, phenomenologists came to view their object as the domain of essences, the essences of directly experienceable things. These essences were to be described, and in their description nothing was to be assumed. At this stage in the development of phenomenology, meanings most clearly resembled Platonic forms.[30]

Phenomenological philosophers were as unwilling as analysts to assimilate their method to that of any of the existing sciences.[31] Phenomenology, thus, could not take advantage of inductive procedures. Induction, it was thought, yielded no certain knowledge. Through induction one discovered what was probably the case, but not what was certainly the case. To find the evidence on the basis of which to transform the phrase

For a crow to be a crow, it must have . . .

into a true sentence, it was thought that inductive means were of no help. Neither could there be appeal to experimental methods. Phenomenologists thought that setting up experimental situations involved assumptions.

At this point in the development of phenomenology essences were viewed as rather extraordinary items. Scientists with their experimental, inductive methods dealt with realms of fact, but phenomenologists dealt with something different and far more important. The sciences could tell various things about birds, for

29. This is most clearly the case, I believe, in Husserl's writings, his Platonistic disavowals notwithstanding. In this connection Husserl's *Ideas* is most relevant.

30. This is not altogether the case, however. See in this connection Herbert Spiegelberg, *The Phenomenological Movement 1* (The Hague, 1960), pp. 85, 96 f.

31. IP 453 ff.

instance, but to locate birds in the first place, to grasp their essence, was the prior task of phenomenology.[32] Only upon successful completion of this task could the various sciences proceed with their work with any degree of conceptual rigor. Phenomenology, it was thought, provided a basis for the sciences, for essences demarcated the world into domains of fact, and only through phenomenology were these essences to be grasped and articulated. Meanings, thus, were given what was virtually a transcendental priority, though only in the work of Husserl's middle period is this clearly and self-consciously asserted.[33]

But what were these meanings and how did one get at them? How, for instance, did one directly experience the essence of jealousy? In this experience what sort of thing was one experiencing? None of these questions was answered well. The second, perhaps, was answered most clearly. The older phenomenologists, Pfänder, Reinach, and Geiger in particular, thought access to essences was gained through a change in attitude toward the specific instances examined.[34] Let us continue with the example of jealousy. The investigator was told to disregard the existence of jealousy, to "bracket" or suspend belief in its existence. What was meant was this: though particular instances were to be considered, it was irrelevant whether appeal was made to actually existing instances. An imagined instance would do. The analyses could not be falsified by the fact that the instances examined did not exist. Further, since phenomenology viewed itself as a noninductive discipline, one instance of jealousy might be all one needed to examine in order to expose jealousy's essence.

The older phenomenologists wanted to know the content of experience, its "what." Questions concerning the "why" of experience, its causal structures and interrelations, were left to the sciences.[35] Phenomenology hoped thus to demarcate a set of questions all its own. What, for instance, made jealousy jealousy and not some-

32. *Ideas* g.18, e.63–64. Curiously enough Heidegger speaks in this way also. See SZ g.8–11, e.28–31.

33. In this connection, see IP 464–71. See also *Ideas,* passim.

34. IP 460 ff.

35. IP 462–63.

thing else? To answer this question the phenomenologist was to detach himself from practical involvement with the instance of jealousy being examined and contemplate it disinterestedly. Only then could the meaning of jealousy be revealed clearly and perspicuously.

One aspect of this understanding of phenomenology seems to me quite correct and philosophically insightful. Since the insight is shared by latter-day phenomenologists as well, I shall term it phenomenological although few analysts would question its validity.

Consider how a philosopher might come to understand the nature of jealousy. Though he might begin by consulting the dictionary definition of the term 'jealousy,' clearly he would go on to consider instances of jealousy to determine whether the dictionary definition was perspicuous enough. Are there invariant characteristics possessed by jealousy which the connotations of common usage do not capture? Are there distinct species of jealousy which are not properly distinguished in common parlance? Are there features in the common understanding of jealousy which are incidental rather than germaine to jealousy, applying to some of its species but not to others? Are there any characteristics at all that are common to all instances of jealousy? A serious philosopher taking jealousy as his subject matter would not stop short of answering all of these questions. To answer them he would of course be compelled to consult experience. He might read *Othello*, observe a colleague known to exhibit jealous behavior when reminded of the work of a rival scholar, remember and contemplate his own jealousy over his brother's new car, and so on. How people spoke in these sorts of situations would be important to him, and a dictionary might be indispensable. But the situations themselves in their extralinguistic dimensions would occupy his attention too. Much like the psychiatrist whose therapeutic endeavors are guided as much by his patient's gestures, actions, facial expressions and posture as by his patient's remarks, the philosopher studying jealousy would be called upon to look as well as listen, observe as well as read. If this point is granted, it must also be granted that situations and objects, experiences and actions, no less than words and phrases, have meaning. To argue that these meanings are analyzable into linguistic meanings is to do violence to the philosophical enterprise, an enterprise which involves more than anything else a judicious and perspicacious examination of experience for the purpose of securing its proper description. No analyst would want to perform such a reduction, for it would deprive him of some indispensable equipment for the successful accomplishment of his philosophical task. Phenomenology makes this equipment the center of its concern. Without recourse to this equipment analysis could not be carried out. This is not sufficiently recognized in analytic philosophy's official doctrines of scope, method, and purpose. Phenomenology, thus, is as necessary to perspicuous analysis as is analysis to perceptive phenomenology. Their respective histories bear this out.

From what has been said it remains unclear precisely what a meaning is. Such, at least, was the fate of the early phenomenologists' conceptions of meaning. Not all of them conceived of meanings Platonically, but their doctrines easily lent themselves to Platonic interpretation. In particular, Husserl's insistence on the separation of fact and essence suggested a third realm whose legal owner was the philosopher.[36] Latter day phenomenologists such as Heidegger, however much they have been influenced by the conception of phenomenology they inherited, have reacted against this view of phenomenology's subject matter.[37] Heidegger, among others, suggests that the meaning of a nonlinguistic entity be understood as that entity's *functions*.[38] Involvement rather than detachment, concern rather than disinterest are counseled as the proper phenomenological attitudes by means of which to reveal and describe these functions.[39] This functionalist doctrine is one with which I agree.

To ask the meaning of events and objects, situations and experiences, I believe, is to ask their function. In this respect the

36. In this connection, see *Ideas* g.91 ff., e.150 ff.

37. See, for instance, SZ g.208, e.251–52; g.147, e.187.

38. This interpretation of Heidegger's position is somewhat controversial. I derive it from Heidegger's conception of *Zuhandenheit* and his insistence on man being understood in terms of man's *Seinkönnen*.

39. SZ g.69, e.98–99, passim.

meaning of nonlinguistic entities resembles the meaning of linguistic entities. In either case, a functionalist account is necessary to describe meaning perspicuously and without falling prey to Platonic commitments. The obvious questions to ask are what sorts of things functions are, whether all functions are meanings, and how things come to have functions. If a philosopher could carefully distinguish the various types of linguistic and nonlinguistic functions, eliminate those, if any, which were not meanings, and account for how the remaining functional types came to be, he would have answered sufficiently the major philosophical questions concerning the nature of meaning.

Something happens to nonlinguistic entities which converts them into functional (meaningful) entities. Their meaningfulness, in fact, cannot be divorced from this happening, for this happening is an indispensable constituent of their functional status. 'Function' is a relative term. Though used in the singular, 'function' presupposes a plural context, i.e. a plurality of related functions from which it derives its own functional status. Any other use of 'function' is highly metaphorical. A web of functions, I believe, is created and maintained in its existence by that happening which was previously dignified with the label 'Being.' What enables a nonlinguistic entity to function is that Being happens to it.

While it makes a great deal of sense to speak of nonlinguistic entities as existing prior to the happening which gives them their functional status, this is not so obviously true of linguistic entities. The happening which gives linguistic entities their meanings (functions) cannot be viewed to be subsequent to the existence of those linguistic entities themselves, at least not unproblematically. 'Language' is an ambiguous term. Most often it means what Wittgensteinians term a *language game*. On this interpretation of 'language' it is an analytic truth that language cannot precede the bestowal of functions upon it. The two are unquestionably simultaneous, because they are in important respects identical. 'Language,' however, might mean those natural elements, the grunts and groans, shrieks and grimaces, out of which some philosophers think language games have developed. In this sense a very sophisticated anthropological theory, buttressed with philosophical arguments, just might convince one that language preceded its functions. But this thesis is very problematic. To argue that grunts and groans, shrieks and grimaces were transformed from merely natural phenomena to elements constitutive of human language is to presuppose that those phenomena were completely nonintentional to begin with. Though this view helps preserve the distinction between man and what the medieval and modern traditions so patronizingly termed 'the brutes,' it does little else and in fact appears to obstruct discussion of the genesis of peculiarly human forms of behavior.

What, then, is meaning? I can now reformulate this question in a more perspicuous way by breaking it up into some separate but closely related questions. What happens to entities by virtue of which they come to have functions? What are functions, and what is the most perspicuous typology that can be given them? How do entities relate to the functions they possess? In particular, what is the relation of linguistic entities to the meanings (functions) they bear? What is the precise relation of the functional status of entities to that which gives them this status? How do functions relate to one another? In particular, how do linguistic functions relate to nonlinguistic functions?

I conclude this chapter with an indication of how I conceive the happening that is Being and the notion of meaning it engenders. An indispensable part of what is meant by 'Being' is a very specific event. The Being of an entity, its meaning, is in part at least that entity's coming into and being maintained in a context of (human) awareness and agency, actual or potential.[40] The meaning of an entity, in other words, is constituted in part by that entity's coming into (human) presence. To ask the question of meaning, then, is to entangle oneself inextricably in the question: What is man? To ask what entities mean is to ask their functions within the broad, diversified, and subtle contexts of human presence, individual and social.

What an entity means *to me* is for the most part how it func-

40. I enclose 'human' in parentheses out of deference to investigations, empirical and philosophical, into the status of nonhuman forms of consciousness, their structures and scope.

tions for me. This in turn depends upon how I understand myself, and this understanding is unavoidably social and communal. Thus when I ask what an entity means *to me* I ask what is in large measure a social or communal question. Its answer, as has already been seen in the case of linguistic functions, cannot be derived from doctrines resurrected from the old and venerable traditions of associationalist psychology. But from where, then, do answers come? Again, what precisely is a function, and how do linguistic and nonlinguistic functions relate? These questions are left unanswered and still other, equally perplexing questions are yet to be formulated. In particular, more needs to be said about language, its philosophical significance, and its import within the context of phenomenology. To these matters I now turn.

CHAPTER 3

Phenomenology and Language

No account of the problems that I wish to clarify through Heidegger can avoid discussion of the phenomenological method of investigation. Explication of this method is difficult, for even among phenomenologists there is considerable controversy over what the method is and does, who actually uses it and whether Heidegger has used it. In the midst of this controversy a few facts are certain: Heidegger took the method seriously in *Being and Time*, claimed to be philosophizing in accordance with it, and offered a detailed interpretation of its significance. He saw the successful use of phenomenology to be inextricably bound up with an adequate understanding and insightful use of language. No other phenomenologist, I believe, has seen this point as clearly, and it is crucial to an accurate understanding of the usefulness of phenomenology. If the problems which concern me are to be clarified, some light must be shed on the meaning of Heidegger's phenomenological method as he alludes to it in pivotal remarks such as these:

> Phenomenology is our way of access to what is to be the theme of ontology, and it is our way of giving it demonstrative precision. *Only as phenomenology is ontology possible.*[1]

> ... our investigation comes up against the fundamental question of philosophy. This is one that must be treated phenomenologically.[2]

> ... we must avoid uninhibited word-mysticism. Nevertheless, the ultimate business of philosophy is to preserve the force of

1. SZ g.35, e.60.
2. SZ g.27, e.49–50.

the most elemental words in which Dasein expresses itself, and to keep the common understanding from levelling them off to that unintelligibility which functions in turn as a source of pseudoproblems.[3]

The business of Heidegger's phenomenology is to uncover phenomena. Two questions arise: What sort of item does Heidegger think a phenomenon *is?* How does he go about uncovering one? After dealing with these questions, I turn to a more specific consideration of language. First I consider its relation to meaning, primarily through a comparison of Heidegger's and Wittgenstein's views on this relation. Then I discuss, extend, and in certain respects endorse some of Heidegger's views, particularly the non-etymological ones, on the use of language in the service of phenomenology. Having evaluated the conception of a "phenomenological" philosophy, I conclude the chapter with a reformulation of the second of my guiding questions: What is the philosophical significance of language?

Toward the beginning of *Being and Time*[4] Heidegger defines the "object" or phenomenon of phenomenology as "that which shows itself in itself." In order to clarify this definition he distinguishes it from a number of meanings of the term 'appearance' *(Erscheinung)* and from the basic meaning of the term 'semblance' *(Schein)*. He makes these distinctions in order to show the dependence of the latter notions upon his conception of the phenomenon. If Heidegger has succeeded in making these distinctions, he has shown not only that phenomena are the foundation stones of our experience, but that phenomenology is a methodological presupposition of any empirically minded discipline that seeks to establish its results with rigor.

Heidegger defines a semblance as "something which shows itself as what in itself it is not."[5] A semblance is something that looks as if it were other in character than it actually is.

Here Heidegger is referring to qualitative as opposed to exis-

3. SZ g.220, e.262.
4. SZ g.27–39, e.49–63. Many of the following remarks will come close to being direct quotes from this section of *Being and Time*.
5. SZ g.28, e.51.

tential seemings. Clearly a variety of phrases are used in referring
to semblances. For instance, one says that a particular tie *looks*
green but in fact is actually blue, or that Smith *seems* bored but
in fact is quite interested in what is going on. In short, to say that
something is a semblance is to say things about it like the following: it looks as if it were, looks to be, seems to be φ, but in fact is
actually not φ. A semblance, thus, is not a quality that something
only seems to have, but the something that only seems to have the
quality.

It is Heidegger's view that only something which gives the pre-
tense of "showing itself" can show itself as something it is not and
thus that the concept of the phenomenon is presupposed by the
concept of semblance.[6] The concept of looking φ, in other words,
presupposes the concept of being φ. The ability to experience something as a semblance presupposes the ability to experience something as a phenomenon. Without the concept of the phenomenon
the concept of a semblance has no meaning.

This distinction need not detain us. Attempts to deny its force
have been given up by all but the most intransigent of sense datum
theorists.[7] Austin, Merleau-Ponty, and others have pointed out the
weaknesses to which the attackers of the distinction fall prey,[8] and
Heidegger's own adherence to the distinction is hardly more than
an expression of philosophical orthodoxy.

Far more important for an understanding of what Heidegger
seeks is the term 'appearance,' to which he assigns three meanings.
Something can "show itself," Heidegger thinks, and in so doing
announce the presence of something else that does not show itself.[9]
Following Heidegger's example, in showing themselves, symptoms
of a disease announce the presence of that disease. What does not
show itself, the disease, is sometimes taken to be the appearance.

6. SZ g.29, e.51.
7. This point need not, I think, be labored. In this connection, see
Wilfred Sellars, *Science, Perception and Reality* (New York, 1963), pp.
60–105. Here Sellars indicates the conceptual absurdities of the sense
datum position and of the "language of appearance" doctrine.
8. See in this connection J. L. Austin, *Sense and Sensibilia* (New
York, 1964).
9. SZ g.29 ff., e.51 ff.

Let us call this meaning of the term 'appearance' appearance$_1$. Subscripts are not in Heidegger's repertoire, but it will nonetheless be helpful to use them. Heidegger defines appearance$_1$ as that which does not show itself but gives indication of its presence through something that does show itself.[10] There are, for instance, diseases which one cannot "see," but which give indication of their presence through symptoms which one does see. In these cases the disease would be called an appearance$_1$. Since an appearance$_1$ can only *appear*—that is to say, give indication of its presence—if something "shows itself," the concept of an appearance$_1$ presupposes the concept of a phenomenon.[11] But this is not to "reduce" theoretical entities to observable phenomena. Such an interpretation of Heidegger's phenomenology would confuse it with phenomenalism. Heidegger's understanding of the relations obtaining between observational and theoretical frameworks is more complex than most neo-Heideggerians suggest.[12]

Heidegger thinks the term 'appearance' can also be taken to mean that which does the announcing, e.g. the symptoms of a disease which announce the presence of that disease. Let us call this meaning of the term 'appearance' appearance$_2$. An appearance$_2$ in Heidegger's view is that which, in its showing of itself, announces the presence of something which does not show itself. To use our example again, by showing themselves the symptoms of a disease, appearances$_2$, announce the presence of that disease, though the disease itself does not show itself. It should be evident that if an appearance$_2$ is to possess a feature, a "reference relationship" *(Verweisungsbezug),* as Heidegger terms it, whereby it can announce or give indication of the presence of something else, an appearance$_2$ must first of all show itself. For something to *be* an appearance$_2$, thus, it must first *be* a phenomenon. The concept of an appearance$_2$ presupposes the concept of a phenomenon. Heidegger

10. SZ g.29, e.52.
11. SZ g.29, e.53.
12. The most influential statement of the neo-Heideggerian position with which I take issue is found, I believe, in Wild's writings. See John Wild, *Existence and the World of Freedom* (Englewood Cliffs, 1965), pp. 80–97.

argues this, again without prejudice to the status of "theoretical" entities.[13]

Finally, Heidegger claims, the term 'appearance' may mean that which shows itself to be an emanation of what it announces but which veils that thing as it is in itself. Let us call this meaning of the term 'appearance' appearance$_3$. Heidegger takes this meaning to be basic to Kant's account of "appearances" (Erscheinungen) in his Critique of Pure Reason. It is not an unduly controversial interpretation of Kant's philosophy to say of Kant's "appearances" that appearances (appearances$_3$) are manifestations of things-in-themselves which reveal those things-in-themselves, but not as they are in themselves. When one contrasts thing-in-itself and appearance$_3$ in this manner one is not talking about two totally different things, but about two different modes of the same thing. In short, the appearance$_3$ is the thing-in-itself in the mode of its being known and, as known, the thing-in-itself takes on a modified structure which obstructs one's comprehension of the same thing-in-itself in any mode of its being which transcends the cognitive situation.[14]

Heidegger contends that here too the notion of the phenomenon is presupposed, for only if something "shows itself" can the notions of "covering" or "veiling" arise.[15] Only if a thing-in-itself manifests itself can it manifest itself other than it is in itself. This is to say that for something to be an appearance$_3$ is for it first to be a phenomenon and that the concept of an appearance$_3$ thus presupposes the concept of a phenomenon.

Much has been made of Heidegger's disagreement with Husserl concerning phenomenology as a philosophical method.[16] Whatever the nature of this disagreement, it does not lie in the distinctions so far examined, particularly not in this last one. Heidegger's remarks concerning appearances$_3$ break no new ground. They simply

13. SZ g.29–31, e.53–54. I say more concerning the status of "theoretical entities" in my "Worlds and World Views," Man and World 2: 228–47.

14. SZ g.30 ff., e.53 ff. It is not altogether clear that Heidegger would be in full agreement with this statement. In this connection see also KB.

15. SZ g.30–31, e.54–55.

16. See Spiegelberg, The Phenomenological Movement 1, pp. 271 ff., as well as IP.

reaffirm the general strategy employed by the phenomenological tradition in its dispute with the neo-Kantianism of the late nineteenth century.[17] After establishing the fundamental character of the phenomenon, the phenomenological tradition tries to show how the distinction between appearance$_3$ and thing-in-itself arises within experience, that is to say, on the basis of an experience of the phenomenon.[18] The tradition then works to remove objections to the basic phenomenological thesis that the thing-in-itself is the phenomenon properly understood and that an appearance$_3$, Kant's appearance, is the phenomenon improperly or deficiently understood.[19] Though Kant's doctrines exert the major influence upon Heidegger, Heidegger's chief adversaries, not only in the Kant book[20] but in *Being and Time,* are clearly the neo-Kantians.

Heidegger does not claim that all entities are reducible to phenomena, though some followers of Heidegger have been impressed with the possibilities of such a reduction.[21] Heidegger only claims that an understanding of any entity presupposes an understanding of phenomena.[22] Nonetheless, if one takes seriously Baumgarten's definition of metaphysics quoted by Heidegger in the Kant book[23] that "metaphysics is the science which contains the first principles of that which is within the comprehension of human knowledge," one can see how phenomenology might come to be understood to be metaphysical in a way which tempts one to a reductionist thesis. Clearly it is more than just a temptation to view phenomenology as a metaphysical method if one follows Baumgarten, which Heidegger obviously does.[24]

17. This is quite evident from the polemic of KB.

18. In this connection SZ g.28 ff., e.51 ff. is most illuminating. Here Heidegger tries to make this case out in a conceptually rigorous way. See also KB g.31 ff., e.30 ff.

19. *Ideas* g.87 ff, e.147 ff.

20. Heidegger's book on Kant develops Heidegger's positive thesis as well. The book is not simply an essay on Kant interpretation.

21. See Wild, *Existence and the World of Freedom,* pp. 41 ff. and pp. 80 ff.

22. SZ g.28 ff., e.51 ff. These passages, however, are not conclusive.

23. KB g.15, e.9–10.

24. Heidegger's remarks on the nature of metaphysics are not altogether consistent. On this point, however, there should be no controversy.

As a discipline, metaphysics is unusually resilient. It manages to have a subterranean life of its own even among the most articulate of its detractors. Writing to Markus Herz concerning the *Critique of Pure Reason,* Kant implies that if the investigations of other philosophers in the tradition are metaphysical, then his work represents the metaphysics of metaphysics. It is not hard to see why Kant says this. Rather than talking about objects, he talks about the conditions which must be satisfied if one is to talk about objects. There is a direct parallel to this in Heidegger's phenomenology. The concept of the phenomenon so far explicated is referred to by Heidegger as the ordinary concept of the phenomenon. It does not designate the phenomenon which is the "object" of his phenomenology.[25] In his terms, an "ordinary" phenomenon is merely *ontic.*

Heidegger understands the phenomenon in a way which he claims to be the true *phenomenological* conception of the phenomenon: as that which already shows itself prior to the phenomenon as ordinarily understood and which accompanies the "ordinary" phenomenon in every case. Let us call such a phenomenon a phenomenon$_H$. Heidegger uses 'prior to' in the Kantian sense of "necessary condition for," and he suggests that Kant's space would be a likely (though losing) candidate for the post of phenomenon$_H$.[26] From this we can draw the following conclusion: if an ordinary phenomenon is anything that can be brought to "show itself"—and this will range us far and wide, from books and benches to a baseball game, an aesthetic experience, a death, in short, to the totality of entities—then a phenomenon$_H$ is a condition which makes possible the "showing of itself" of any of these ordinary phenomena. Heidegger claims that a phenomenon$_H$ shows itself unthematically, but that it can be brought to show itself explicitly and systematically.[27] It is the business of his phenomenology to bring phenomena$_H$ to show themselves in this explicit and systematic way.

25. SZ g.31, e.54–55. Undercutting metaphysics is clearly one of Heidegger's major preoccupations after the writing of *Being and Time.* In *Being and Time,* however, his attitude toward metaphysics appears to be ambivalent.

26. SZ g.31, e.54–55.

27. SZ g.35 ff., e.59 ff.

In Heidegger's view it is only because one has an awareness of phenomena_H that one can have an awareness of ordinary phenomena. Although we are always dimly aware of phenomena_H, our attention, he thinks, is for the most part directed toward ordinary phenomena. Therefore, it takes a certain refocusing on our part, a certain reflective turn, to make phenomena_H objects of our thematic (explicit) awareness. To Heidegger's thinking this refocusing is no simple matter. It involves the attainment of what he terms 'authenticity' (*Eigentlichkeit*).[28] The attainment of this authenticity, Heidegger thinks, is at the same time what opens one toward Being.[29] It is here that we make connection with our discussion of the first two chapters, for the relation obtaining between phenomena_H and Being is most intimate. Heidegger's view is this: phenomena_H in their structural interconnections *constitute* Being, and that about them which can be disclosed constitutes the meaning (functions) of Being.[30] It is precisely this that binds phenomenology and ontology together in Heidegger's thought and makes Heidegger a professed phenomenologist.

The articulation of the guidelines for refocusing constitutes the so-called "existential" dimension of Heidegger's philosophy, which it is the task of *Being and Time* to explicate. However, refocusing, rather than being an end in itself, is an activity engaged in for the sake of that which is to be focused upon. To argue that Heidegger is at bottom an existentialist is to miss this point. Obvious similarities between Heidegger's early subject matter and, say, Kierkegaard's or Nietzsche's concerns have tended to obscure for many interpreters the less obvious but nonetheless crucial differences. It is these differences which make Heidegger a fruitful means of access to the questions I wish to reformulate.

The aim of Heidegger's phenomenology is bringing about a certain refocusing and articulating its content. If the study of ordinary phenomena satisfies Baumgarten's definition of metaphysics, Heidegger's phenomenology might be thought of as the metaphysics of metaphysics. More true to Heidegger's way of expressing

28. SZ g.31, e.54–55; g.35 ff., e.59 ff. See especially chapter four.
29. In this connection, see EIM g.14–17, e.15–18.
30. SZ g.37, e.61.

himself, it tries to overcome metaphysics, to go beyond metaphysics, to go back into the ground of metaphysics. But whether Heidegger actually thought of what he was doing in these terms when he wrote *Being and Time* is doubtful. The book is not as methodologically self-conscious as Heidegger later suggests—a fact which is largely responsible for the distinction made between the earlier and the later Heidegger.[31] This methodological hesitancy is also the source of the self-admitted turn *(Kehre)* in Heidegger's thought which takes place shortly after the writing of *Being and Time*.[32]

A look at a particular phenomenon$_H$ should clarify the notion further. The phenomenon$_H$ I shall consider Heidegger calls *world*.[33] It is a particularly important phenomenon, for a number of writers on Heidegger come to identify it with Being itself.[34] Consider the following statements, which employ 'world' in a Heideggerian way:

> They live in two different *worlds*.
> When she died his whole *world* crumbled.
> He lives in a strange *world*.

These statements suggest a perfectly respectable use of 'world' which allows one to make the following true statement: 'When I die, my world dies with me.' Statements of this nature abound in common parlance. Wittgenstein has something like this in mind when he says in the *Tractatus* (6.431) 'So too at death the world does not alter, but comes to an end.'

In Heidegger's view, using the term 'world' in this way does not commit one to idealism.[35] Heidegger believes he has avoided traditional idealism because 'world' as it is now being used refers to an

31. For a discussion of this distinction, see W. J. Richardson, *Heidegger Through Phenomenology to Thought* (The Hague, 1963), pp. viii–xxiii; pp. 209 ff.

32. This clearly is a matter of interpretation. In this connection, see Richardson, *Heidegger*, pp. xvi ff.

33. SZ g.63 ff., e.91 ff.

34. In this connection, see John Wild, "An English Version of Martin Heidegger's *Being and Time*," *Review of Metaphysics* 16 (December 1962): 311 ff.

35. SZ g.205–08, e.249–52. Clearly Heidegger cannot be classified as an idealist in any traditional sense of that term.

entity of a different "logical" type than the type which characterizes entities which are "within" or simply "in" the world. The conceptual behavior of these two types, he thinks, is different. The world and entities within the world cannot be mapped by means of the same conceptual geography—a statement which translates Heidegger's assertion that the ontological is conceptually different from the ontic. The entities within one's world, thus, are not jeopardized by the fact that one's death involves the death of one's world too.[36]

Before turning to a more positive characterization of our phenomenon$_H$ I wish to clear up a certain ambiguity.[37] When reference is made to *the* world—and since it is a phenomenon$_H$ I shall refer to it as the world$_H$—reference is being made not to any particular person's particular world$_H$, but to the structures of anyone's world$_H$, which, it is presumed, are the same as the structures of anyone else's world$_H$. When reference is made to *my* world$_H$, as opposed to *the* world$_H$, reference is being made only to my particular world$_H$. As should be obvious, it is *the* world$_H$ that matters philosophically. Heidegger sees this and makes the distinction I have just presented.[38] A denial of this distinction, it is clear, has as its consequence a solipsism which is hardly avoidable. Leaving Heidegger aside, the philosophical point is this: one need only to attend to the logic of such statements as 'My world is falling to pieces' to realize that they presuppose for their sense an extrapersonal notion of world. With this admission, solipsism becomes untenable.

The world$_H$ is in certain ways akin to Kant's space. In the *Critique of Pure Reason* Kant presents the following argument to establish space as a pure intuition and, thus, as a necessary condition for the possibility of experience:[39] experiences of various regions of space

36. SZ g.63–66, e.91–95; g.211 ff., e.254 ff.

37. John Wild points up this ambiguity. See Wild "An English Version," *Review of Metaphysics:* 311–12.

38. Wild would clearly take issue with me on this point. His article in the *Review of Metaphysics* presents his case admirably well.

39. Kant, *Kritik der Reinen Vernunft* (Hamburg, 1956), g.66–67, e.67–68 (A23–24, B38–39). The English edition I refer to is the Kemp Smith translation. See Kant, *Critique of Pure Reason,* trans. Kemp Smith (New York, 1965). Hereafter cited as KdRv.

and of various spatial relations cannot be the building blocks out of which the notion of space as a whole is constructed, for if one is to think the parts at all, one can think of them only as being in the whole. Hence one already has some notion of the whole. To experience a spatial region or relation *as* a spatial region or relation presupposes the whole of space as that in terms of or within which one experiences the region *as* a region or the relation *as* a relation.

Now Heidegger holds that anything one encounters is encountered as being *within* one's world$_H$.[40] To experience something *as* something is to experience and interpret that something in terms of one's world$_H$. Had one no world$_H$, one would have no cognitive experience at all. Thus one's world$_H$ serves as a necessary condition for the possibility of one's experience, and *the* world$_H$ is a necessary condition for the possibility of anyone's experience. Phenomena$_H$ are to this extent amenable to Kantian interpretation. A more precise statement would perhaps be this: any given phenomenon$_H$ is a structural moment of the one and only true phenomenon$_H$, namely, Being, and Being has a transcendental status. In short, to articulate the totality of phenomena$_H$ in their structural interconnections is to reveal the meaning (functions) of Being. Such is Heidegger's view.[41]

Unfortunately the analogy with Kant's space breaks down. In the first place, the part–whole relationship sustained between the parts of space and the whole of space would be a misleading way of characterizing the relationship between an entity within one's world$_H$ and one's world$_H$ itself. For Heidegger one's world$_H$ is not an entity of the same "logical" type as that of the entities which fall within it. The same conceptual map cannot represent them both. Thus the entities which are within one's world$_H$ cannot be said to be parts of one's world. To use Heidegger's post–*Being and Time* terminology, to think of them in this way would be to fail to think the ontological difference *as* difference.[42] Being and its structures

40. In this connection see SZ g.363–64, e.414–15.

41. Heidegger does not appeal to the term 'function.' His term is 'involvement' *(Bewandtnis)*. Other terms such as 'potentiality-for-Being' *(Seinkönnen)* also indicate the validity of my functional interpretation.

42. In this connection, see ID.

would be reduced to the status of entities and their characteristics. For Heidegger one's world$_H$ is simply an "in terms of which" and everything a person experiences is experienced in terms of it.[43]

The analogy with Kant's space breaks down in a second way. Part of Kant's argument in the Transcendental Aesthetic[44] is directed against the Leibnizian stratagem of construing the 'in' in which things are said to be *in* space in terms of the 'in' of class inclusion, Kant argues that the way things are *in* space is not analyzable in terms of the logical relation of class inclusion. Now for Heidegger the way entities are *in* one's world$_H$ is not to be construed either in terms of the logical 'in' of class inclusion or the spatial 'in' of spatial withinness. The entities which one encounters as being *in* one's world$_H$, Heidegger thinks, are "in" that world$_H$ in a way most closely analogous to and most clearly indicated by the way the term 'in' functions in the following statements, which I shall arbitrarily designate as statements exemplifying an "existential" use of 'in.'[45] (This terminology is foreign to Heidegger.)

> Dick is *in* a terrible predicament.
> Harry is all wrapped up *in* his work.
> Tom is *in* marine biology.

In Heidegger's view, for an entity to be *in* one's world$_H$ is for it to be an "object" of one's concern.[46] Heidegger construes such seemingly innocent acts as "just looking at something" or "just thinking about something" as ways of being concerned with that something and in most cases degenerate ways of being concerned.[47]

But what then *is* one's world$_H$? For Heidegger it is the structure of one's concern.[48] It is those structures which make possible one's being concerned with the entities with which one is concerned. It is what makes human agency and awareness—in short, human pre-

43. SZ g.192, e.236–37; g.221, e.264.
44. KdRv g.68, e.69 (A24–25, B39).
45. Heidegger's use of the term existential (*existenzial*) does not altogether accord with this usage I have adopted, but there are close connections.
46. SZ g.54 ff., e.79 ff.
47. SZ g.56–57, e.83–84; g.59 ff., e.86 ff.
48. In this connection Heidegger's remarks concerning Care (*Sorge*) and significance (*Bedeutsamkeit*) are of great importance. See SZ.

sence—possible. Since the basic way in which one experiences entities is in being concerned with them, the structures of one's world$_H$ are *the* necessary conditions for the possibility of one's experience.[49] From the standpoint of *Being and Time,* these structures are manifest in all one's dealings with the objects of one's concern, but in his natural attitudes a man's very concern with the objects of his concern focuses his attention away from the structures of the concern itself.[50] As a remedy for this situation Heidegger does not suggest introspection; this would be but another species of concern, self-concern.[51] Rather, he points to certain basic experiences which bring these structures to the fore.[52] Beyond this, he suggests certain uses of language as means of conceptually fixing the structures so revealed. Heidegger believes that these structures constitute the world$_H$ which is a phenomenon$_H$, and if some commentators are correct, *the* phenomenon$_H$.[53] These structures are neither more nor less mysterious than Kant's categories and in Heidegger's estimation they are much more concrete.[54] By saying this I hope to reiterate and underscore the unmistakable Kantian ring of Heidegger's phenomena$_H$ when seen from the standpoint of *Being and Time.*

Much has been, and probably will continue to be, written about the puzzling and complex philosophical relationship between Heidegger's and Husserl's phenomenologies.[55] I have already mentioned the concern of both men to attack neo-Kantian notions of an unknowable entity. There is another dimension of this relationship that merits our attention in the present context. Heidegger writes:

49. This thesis requires the partial identification of *Sein* and *Welt.* See SZ g.37–39, e.61–63; g.63 ff., e.91 ff.

50. SZ g.129, e.167; g.172, e.216–17; g.192, e.236–37. See also g.89 ff., e.122 ff.

51. SZ g.212, e.255–56; g.207–08, e.250–52.

52. SZ g.231–35, e.274–78.

53. Here the philosopher I have primarily in mind is John Wild. A view quite close to this is held by Vycinas. See Vincent Vycinas, *Earth and Gods* (The Hague, 1961).

54. KB g.219–22, e.251–55; SZ g.8 ff., e.28 ff.

55. In this connection, see IP. See also Spiegelberg, *The Phenomenological Movement* 1, pp. 257 ff.

As my familiarity with phenomenology grew, no longer merely through literature but by actual practice, the question about Being, aroused by Brentano's work, nevertheless remained always in view. So it was that doubt arose whether the "thing itself" was to be characterized as intentional consciousness, or even as the transcendental ego. If, indeed, phenomenology, as the process of letting things manifest themselves, should characterize the standard method of philosophy, and if from ancient times the guide-question of philosophy has perdured in the most diverse forms as the question about the Being of beings, then Being had to remain the first and last thing-itself of thought. Meanwhile "phenomenology" in Husserl's sense was elaborated into a distinctive philosophical position according to a pattern set by Descartes, Kant and Fichte. The historicity of thought remained completely foreign to such a position.[56]

If we take Heidegger's words seriously, the phenomenology of *Being and Time* differs from Husserl's practice of the method less in the method itself than in the "object" towards which the method is directed. For Heidegger, the "object" is Being. If one keeps in mind Heidegger's repeated insistence in *Being and Time* that the structures to be grasped phenomenologically are "equiprimordial" (*gleichursprünglich*),[57] that the world (in our terminology, the world$_H$) is constituted by a multiplicity of structures, and that the world is a phenomenon in the proper phenomenological sense (a phenomenon$_H$), it is not difficult to see how Being might come to be identified with the world$_H$. This is nonetheless a problematic identification, for Heidegger does not explicitly make it in *Being and Time*, and it is not clear that he wished to make it. Here I simply want to point out the ground for the intimate connection between the notions of Being and world$_H$.

In *Being and Time* the phenomenon$_H$ is Being itself and thus (problematically) the world (world$_H$), which (again problematically) is identical with Being in a manner as yet unclarified in Hei-

56. Richardson, *Heidegger*, pp. xii–xv.
57. SZ g.41, e.65; g.220, e.263; g.271, e.316.

degger's thinking. To say that this identification is not made and
that it therefore remains problematic is to point up a difficulty we
have met with before in different guise.[58] If the formulation of the
doctrine of meaning is left ambiguous in *Being and Time,* the notion of world is left equally so. In *Being and Time,* Heidegger appears first to view the world (world$_H$) as a structure of man's
(Dasein's) Being, then as man's Being itself.[59] This course can
only lead to the solipsistic tendencies of subjective or critical idealism. When he argues against traditional forms of idealism, therefore, the world begins to lose these moorings and reaches out to
attach to Being itself.[60] Thus world, no less than meaning, is left
problematic. Questions concerning each need careful formulation
in the light of the philosophical problems these notions suggest.

Knowledge of Being, finally, is *transcendental knowledge,* and if
a Kantian interpretation of Heidegger's thought is insufficient for
the explanation of this transcendentality, it is nonetheless a first
step that must be taken and that Heidegger takes.[61]

The function of language within Heidegger's phenomenological
method is the key to an understanding of how Heidegger thinks
phenomena$_H$ are to be uncovered. The key passage in this regard
is the following:

> we must avoid uninhibited word-mysticism. Nevertheless, the
> ultimate business of philosophy is to preserve the force of the
> most elemental words in which Dasein expresses itself, and to
> keep the common understanding from levelling them off to
> that unintelligibility which functions in turn as a source of
> pseudo-problems.[62]

58. See p. 46 ff.

59. See in this connection the puzzling section in SZ entitled "the
temporality of Being-in-the-world and the problem of the transcendence of
the world" (SZ g.350 ff., e.401 ff.). Clearly my remarks concerning Heidegger's conception of the "world" are interpretive and rather controversial.
They are, I believe, nonetheless accurate.

60. For Heidegger's argument against traditional idealism, see SZ
g.206 ff, e.250 ff.

61. SZ g.31, e.54–55; g.35–38, e.59–63. See also KB g.208 ff., e.239 ff.

62. SZ g.220, e.262.

This manifesto is both odd and revealing. It sounds like the pronouncement of a linguistic analyst in its insistence on the linguistic origins of some philosophical (pseudo) problems. The therapeutic appeal to language is most odd indeed, for in other contexts Heidegger says that the ultimate task of the philosopher is to reveal and describe phenomena_H, the structures of Being.[63] By preserving the force of certain elemental words Heidegger believes he has obtained access to phenomena_H. One might summarize the entire program and method of *Being and Time* by the statement that phenomena_H are the items to be gotten *at,* and that the preservation of the force of certain elemental words is the means of getting at them.

The burden placed upon language here is staggering. One cannot but wonder whether a philosophical appeal to language can be at once both therapeutic and, in a metaphysical sense, constructive. Doesn't such an appeal become whimsical and speculative, and if so, then in what sense is the appeal a therapeutic one? Unfortunately, the difficulties involved in answering these questions are compounded by the fact that Heidegger's understanding and use of 'language' (and language itself) in *Being and Time* are not altogether consistent.

In *Being and Time,* "preserving the elemental force of a word" is something like "doing etymology." About this practice and its purpose and justification we know at least the following from our previous analyses and interpretations:[64] Heidegger believes that the fundamental concepts by means of which Western man philosophizes have sprung from the Greek language and have their proper residence in that language. The terms embodying these concepts have of course been translated into Latin, and subsequently into German, French and English. Heidegger thinks that to be comprehended properly in their significance for philosophy, however, these terms must be traced back to the Greek. He does not appear to hold that philosophical terms mean only what the Greeks understand them to mean. Rather he thinks that a careful examination of the context and circumstances out of which these terms came into actual use will aid us in understanding the various extended, qualified,

63. SZ g.34–38, e.58–63.
64. See p. 7 ff.

and almost always technical roles that these terms have come to play in the highly developed contemporary language games into which they enter and thereby become our concern. Since words never free themselves from their etymological ancestry, this etymological method of approach is necessary. Finally, Heidegger appeals to etymology for revisionary as opposed to descriptive purposes. Along with Austin, he thinks that embedded in our language are certain models which exercise a covert control over our thinking. Words that derive their force from these models snare us. In particular Heidegger thinks that we are victims of a certain model for understanding Being, a model drawn from the realm of time concepts. It is this understanding and the model it employs that serves as the focus for Heidegger's etymological analysis.

It will be helpful to look at two more examples of Heidegger's philosophical use of language—occasions on which he believes he has preserved the elemental force of a word through etymological analysis and thereby gained access to phenomena$_H$. One of them is from Greek, one from German.[65]

Consider first Heidegger's analysis of the German term *'in.'* He claims that it is derived from *'innan,'* which means "to reside," "to dwell." The preterit of *'innan,'* viz., *'an,'* means "to be accustomed to," "to be familiar with," "to look after." The overtone is that of "caring for" in each case. Thus the term *'in'* has the basic meaning of "dwelling with those things with which one is familiar and looking after them caringly."[66]

This basic meaning of *'in'* has primary application to man (Dasein) on Heidegger's view. It indicates the way man is in the world, viz., as a being who dwells with those things he is familiar with and looks after them caringly.[67] The preservation of the force of the word *'in'* thus opens the philosopher to the basic phenomena$_H$ which comprise the structure of man's intentionality or directedness toward what is other than himself. Heidegger thinks that by preserving the force of this word he has brought into preliminary focus the phenomena$_H$ which are structural ingredients of man's

65. EIM g.43, e.47.
66. SZ g.54, e.80.
67. SZ g.54–55, e.79–81.

openness to or fundamental posture toward entities within his world$_H$.[68] Since for Heidegger this openness is the world$_H$ itself, what is actually focused upon is the world$_H$ as seen from a slightly different perspective, a perspective which highlights certain of its equiprimordial structures.

Here we must pause to note an obvious objection. One cannot help but wonder whether Heidegger is able to defend himself against the charge of caprice in offering this relatively abstract methodological suggestion. Though 'in' might have what has just been attributed to it as *one* of its meanings, surely the term has many other meanings too. What sense is there in saying, as Heidegger does, either that the meaning just traced is basic or that all other meanings in some way presuppose it?

Here I offer an argument which, though not explicit in Heidegger, is consistent with other of his remarks; construe it as a defense of his position. Consider the meaning of the term 'in' (switching now to English for purposes of exposition) exemplified in such statements as

> The cheese is *in* the refrigerator.
> The pencil is *in* the drawer.
> The desk has been stored *in* the basement.

Only for a being such as man who is *in* the world Heideggerianly does this use of the term 'in' have a meaning. He can grasp this meaning only because he can take up a relation to things which exemplify spatial withinness, and he can take up this relation only because he has an understanding of himself as a being who is (again, Heideggerianly) *in* his world$_H$.

This should give some indication of the transcendental lines along which a justification of a meaning as a basic meaning might proceed. One argument suffices, since all I wish to point out is that Heidegger is not capricious. If there is madness, there is nonetheless method too.

The problems surrounding Heidegger's understanding of language in *Being and Time* are more sharply focused in his contro-

68. In this connection, see SZ g.133, e.171; g.170, e.214; g.350, e.401–02.

versial appeal to the Greek term 'λογος.' This term is of special interest because here again a number of writers on Heidegger see a close connection with Being. They claim in fact that he comes to identify 'λογος' and Being.[69] The reasons for this conjectured identification are not hard to surmise. In the *An Introduction to Metaphysics* Heidegger probes into the meaning of 'λογος' on the basis of an etymological analysis of the infinitive verb form 'λεγειν.' 'Γεγειν,' he claims, means "to put one thing with another," "to gather and yet mark off," "to collect." The notions of order and rank are presupposed. Heidegger holds that 'λογος' refers to a "collecting collectedness," a "primal gathering principle" itself permanently dominant. Heidegger says in fact that the λογος is the "steady gathering," "the intrinsic togetherness" of entities, which he identifies with the Greek notion of Being.[70] Though these analyses purport to offer nothing more than a descriptive account of the Greek model for the understanding of Being, it is not hard to draw a close connection with Heidegger's own, more revisionary remarks about Being. Γογος surely begins to look like some sort of a happening, not itself an entity, in some ways akin to something living, emerging and enduring, which happens only with respect to entities and happens with respect to every entity.

In *Being and Time* Heidegger claims that the basic meaning of 'λογος' is *Rede,* which in the English edition appears as 'discourse.' Discourse for Heidegger is *not* language, and is thus neither written nor spoken. Rather, in some peculiar way, it is that which makes language possible.[71] To bring out this position more clearly I shall resort to the hyphenated phrase, 'intelligibility-articulation.'

Heidegger claims that 'λογος' gets translated by the tradition sometimes as 'reason,' sometimes as 'concept,' 'ground,' or 'judgment.' "Intelligibility-articulation," however, is the basic meaning of 'λογος.' Whenever other meanings are brought to the fore, this basic meaning is presupposed. He claims that 'λογος' means: the making manifest or bringing out into the open of what is to be

69. See, for instance, Richardson, *Heidegger,* pp. 608–10. See also Vycinas, *Earth and Gods,* passim.

70. EIM g.98 ff., e.108 ff.

71. SZ g.32–34, e.55–58; g.271, e.316. See also g.161 ff., e.203 ff.

discussed in such a way that everything that comes to be said about what is to be discussed is drawn from what is to be discussed itself.[72]

To say that the distinguishing "characteristic" of man is his λογος, then, is to say that man is that being who can bring himself into the presence of something in such a way that what he says about that something can be derived from that something itself. In short, Heidegger holds that man is the being who can make himself present to something. At this point, however, Heidegger's position takes a peculiar turn. One is tempted to say that the uniqueness of man consists in his ability to come into the presence of something in such a way as to be able to say anything at all, in his capacity to "speak"—in short, in his possession of language itself. Heidegger however rejects such a formulation. To Heidegger the formulation overlooks the basic meaning of 'λογος' and thereby closes one off from an understanding of those basic acts which make language itself possible.[73] It is only a being who can bring himself into the presence of something or at least find himself in the presence of something who can say anything at all, who can be said to have language in any meaningful sense. If one simply says that man is the being with speech or with language, one is cut off from those basic phenomena_H on the basis of which language itself arises. Heidegger's claim, thus, is that through a subtle scrutiny of language one can reveal certain structures, phenomena_H as we have termed them, which in that peculiar Kantian sense are *prior to* language, and which, rather than being conditioned by language, themselves condition language.

The elemental force of the Greek term 'λογος,' then, when preserved, opens the philosopher to the cluster of phenomena_H that center in and make possible the "coming into the presence of something." Heidegger thinks that there is a basic articulation of one's situation which gets *expressed* in language in such a way that by an examination of language it is possible to grasp the structural determination of one's situation, thereby revealing the constitutive elements of any possible experience. Because language expresses the intelligibility-articulation of a situation, Heidegger thinks its

72. SZ g.32, e.55–56.
73. See in this connection SZ g.165, e.208–09.

structures are analogous to the structures of this intelligibility-articulation and that an examination of the one will yield insight into the other.[74]

Whatever the merits or demerits of this position, the usual argument against it seems to me lacking in force. A philosopher holding this view is often challenged to state and describe those structures which transcend language. Once he has stated and described them it is then pointed out that language was employed in this process. Further grammatical parallels are exhibited which are said to be the covert source of the characteristics attributed to the presumed structures. Thus, it is argued, the structures are not extralinguistic after all. This argument, however, fails to take seriously the consequences of ascribing intentionality to language. If language is, as philosophers claim, intentional in nature, and no items in the universe are in principle unknowable, then various structures should be describable in language. Language should, in describing these structures perspicuously, mirror their characteristics in some of its grammatical properties. This is not an argument for the picture theory of meaning. If there are structures which get expressed in language but are themselves extralinguistic, the verification of their existence must perforce take one beyond simple linguistic analysis. At this point material modes of speech become necessary. This is primarily what distinguishes the phenomenological enterprise from linguistic analysis and makes phenomenology slightly more empirical in its methodological commitments and less idealistic in orientation.

Heidegger's position in this regard falls in a certain sense within the pale of orthodoxy. He is in agreement with those who say that the limits of one's language are the limits of one's world, that "language contributes to the formation and participates in the constitution of fact."[75] Heidegger puts this point in a different way, however. He says that language is "the House of Being."[76] Hei-

74. SZ g.220, e.262; g.160 ff., e.203 ff.

75. Friedrich Waismann, "Verifiability," *Logic and Language*, p. 148.

76. Clearly the use of poetic language complicates the task of interpreting Heidegger's philosophy immeasurably. With regard to viewing language as the "House of Being," see EIM g.11, e.11.

degger falls, thus, within the camp of those who hold that one cannot get outside of one's language to compare its structure with the structure of things—a view adopted by many contemporary philosophers from Wittgenstein to the phenomenological Sartre.[77]

When someone says that he cannot get outside of language to compare it with things, however, he is using the term 'language' in a most unordinary way. The doctrine that one cannot get outside of one's language is in fact a paradoxical doctrine. As one ordinarily understands the term 'language' one is getting outside of it all the time.[78] The very fact that the metalinguistic vocabulary of ordinary language allows for the distinction between a real and a nominal definition indicates this. Observant parents—indefatigable empiricists that they are forced to be—find this truth out in more simple ways. When someone says that he cannot transcend language, he is using 'language' in a way which more closely resembles Heidegger's interpretation of 'λογος' as "intelligibility-articulation." In fact 'language' functions in Waismann's statement to mean something close to what Heidegger means by 'λογος.' Heidegger himself sometimes uses 'language' in this way. For instance:

> words and language are not wrappings in which things are packed for the commerce of those who write and speak. It is in words and language that things first come into being and are.[79]

That Heidegger uses 'language' in a way sometimes equivalent to the term 'λογος' and sometimes not is a further effect of the ambiguity surrounding the concept of meaning.

Language thus is so central an element in Heidegger's appropriation and use of the phenomenological method that, without a proper understanding of it, phenomenology itself becomes impossible. Being (world$_H$) in its "equiprimordial" structures is the phenomenon, and through a certain understanding and analysis of language it is to be uncovered. If it remains unclear at this point as to how the method works, the role of language is bound to become a more explicit theme for inquiry. This, as might be ex-

---

77. Schmitt refers to this as the nontranscendence thesis. See IP 471 ff.
78. In this connection, see IP, especially pp. 472 ff.
79. EIM g.11, e.11.

pected, is what happens in the writings following *Being and Time*.[80]

Let me comment briefly in this connection on the controversial turn in Heidegger's thought which is supposed to have taken place shortly after the writing of *Being and Time*. It is said to justify those discussions of the earlier versus the later Heidegger which parallel in many ways the discussions of Wittgenstein's philosophical development. The extent and significance of the turn are difficult to gauge. Heidegger himself admits a reversal in his thought. He claims however that the turn results from his staying with the basic problem of *Being and Time* and moving to its (unpublished and perhaps unwritten) section entitled "Time and Being." This means that the reversal is inherent in the problem of Being itself and is required if Heidegger is to stay with his subject matter. Heidegger claims that a distinction between the earlier and the later Heidegger—Heidegger I and Heidegger II—is only legitimate if two things are kept in mind: "only by way of what Heidegger I has thought does one gain access to what is to-be-thought by Heidegger II. But [the thought of] Heidegger I becomes possible only if it is contained in Heidegger II."[81]

If Heidegger can be taken seriously, a number of inferences can be drawn concerning the methodological dimension of his concern in *Being and Time*, which is our primary expository concern in this chapter. Three are of particular interest.

(1) The phenomenological method as described in *Being and Time* is an indispensable instrument which must be used if the question of the meaning of Being is to be approached properly, the distinction between earlier and later Heidegger notwithstanding. Though its use is not in itself sufficient for the solution of Heidegger's problem, an acceptance of the method is a necessary first step. Consider in this connection Heidegger's remark in the preface to the seventh edition of *Being and Time*:

While the previous editions have borne the designation "First Half," this has now been deleted. After a quarter of a century,

80. In this connection, see Richardson, *Heidegger*, pp. 259 ff.
81. Ibid., pp. xvi ff., xxii–xxiii.

the second half could no longer be added unless the first were to be presented anew. *Yet the road it has taken is a necessary one.*[82]

(2) If the phenomenological dimension of *Being and Time* rests upon something which makes the phenomenological dimension itself possible, a complete understanding of the phenomenological method cannot be gained from the perspective of *Being and Time* itself. Any formulation and working out of the method in this work is necessarily tentative. In fact throughout *Being and Time* Heidegger insists upon this very tentativity. Toward the end of the published portion of *Being and Time,* Heidegger alludes to a later section he is yet to write, but which does not in fact get written:

> a fully adequate existential interpretation of science cannot be carried out until the *meaning of Being and the connection* between *Being* and *truth* have been clarified in terms of the temporality of existence. The following deliberations are preparatory to the understanding of *this central problematic,* within which, moreover, the idea of phenomenology, as distinguished from the preliminary conception of it which we indicated by way of introduction will be developed for the first time.[83]

Furthermore, if language is as important an element in the employment of the method as Heidegger indicates, then the emphasis on language which occurs in the later writings must be understood as the very working out of the method rather than as its abandonment. Heidegger has little to say about language and λογος in *Being and Time,* and what he does say is not altogether consistent. This may be because he had not yet thought through the significance of these two notions.

(3) It has been claimed that not one but two distinct changes occurred in Heidegger's thought.[84] First, the perspective is modified;

82. SZ g.v, e.17.
83. SZ g.357, e.408.
84. See James Demske, *Sein, Mensch und Tod: Das Todesproblem Bei Martin Heidegger* (Freiburg, 1963), pp. 93 ff.

second, the relation between man and Being is altered. Let us look for a moment at the first of these changes. It is commonly held that the change in perspective involves looking at matters from the standpoint of Being rather than from that of man. Heidegger himself concurs in this judgment.[85] Odd as this surely sounds, a coherent interpretation of this change in perspective is possible. However, to give this interpretation maximum credibility a missing premise must be added which itself has a ring of oddity.

For Heidegger, reflexivity—in particular self-relatedness in the form of self-awareness—is a basic and ontologically indispensable structural element of man.[86] This is to say that reflexivity is one of the characteristics of man's Being. Man is aware of himself however only insofar as there is a situation in terms of which and within the confines of which he has, and in some peculiar sense is, this awareness.[87] Self-awareness is not immediate, but mediated; this is an ontological truth which enters into the constitution of man's Being.

Granting the "ontological" point concerning man, it follows that a situation cannot be brought into existence by man himself. It precedes him in the sense of being a necessary condition for his existence as a being who has an awareness of himself as bound up in a situation. Yet, on the other hand, a situation can only be a situation insofar as there is man. In Heidegger's view it is in terms of what I have called the world$_H$, a structure of man's Being, that entities are encountered as in any sense "meaningful."[88] Only a complex of meaningfully interrelated entities, Heidegger thinks, can give rise to such a thing as a situation.[89]

In *Being and Time* the perspective is man (Dasein) in at least two important ways. First, the attempt is made to bring man into a peculiar sort of encounter with himself through which his concern can be refocused in the direction of Being, and the phenomenological method can be utilized to articulate the structures of Being.

85. See in this connection Heidegger's preface to Richardson, *Heidegger*.
86. See, for instance, SZ g.7, e.26–27.
87. SZ g.220 ff., e.262 ff.
88. See in this connection SZ g.64 ff., e.92 ff.; g.365, e.416–17.
89. By 'situation' I make reference to Heidegger's notion of a *Lage* as opposed to the more technical term *'Situation.'* See SZ g.68, e.97.

Being and Time is thus viewed, at least by the later Heidegger, as an attempt to bring man to philosophy (the study of Being) and not as philosophy (the study of Being) itself.[90] In this respect *Being and Time* resembles in some important ways Hegel's *Phenomenology of Spirit*. Second, the program of *Being and Time* is to work through language to what lies at its base: λογος, which is just another perspective from which to discuss the world_H or Being. The "later" Heidegger, however, having arrived at this base, works back from λογος in an attempt to bring λογος into proper linguistic formulation.[91] But λογος is the basic articulation of the intelligibility of a situation. Hence it constitutes the situation as such and thereby makes man *as* man possible as the being who *expresses* this intelligibility in language. Hence again, to arrive at the λογος is to have arrived at Being and to be in a position to speak from its standpoint. The turn in Heidegger's thought, thus, is dictated by the problem of Being as he sees it in *Being and Time* and is but a working out of that book's insights.

I turn now to a consideration of language in its relation to meaning. Meaning, as we have seen, presents peculiar problems. There are two disparate tendencies with respect to the interpretation of the notion in *Being and Time*. The first of these, which is developed by Heidegger himself in later writings, understands meaning to be Being itself insofar as it can be disclosed—Being insofar as Being can be articulated with respect to its structural moments. The second, the *ing* as opposed to the *ed* interpretation, understands Being to be the disclosing of Being. This disclosing in turn is understood to be the special prerogative of human beings, and thus meaning is construed as a property of man (Dasein). As I have indicated, the doctrine of meaning to which I shall hold is the *ed* doctrine, namely, that meaning is Being itself insofar as Being can be disclosed. On my interpretation Being, which I shall refer to alternatively as the totality of phenomena_H in their interrelations, is in part at least a context of human awareness and agency, of human

90. Heidegger's preface to Richardson's book indicates this, I believe, as does SZ g.v, e.17.

91. In this connection, see Heidegger, *Unterwegs zur Sprache* (Pfullingen, 1959).

presence, into which entities can enter. At the minimum, then, to speak of the meaning of Being is to refer to this context. Specifically, it is to refer to this context insofar as its constituent elements can be conceptually articulated. These constituent elements, I hold, are various functions (meanings) of Being. This might suggest that Being is, after all, a property of man and thus that the *ing* doctrine of meaning is correct. I reject this view, however, though I cannot clarify the reasons for this rejection until later. Suffice it to say that the *ing* doctrine could only be true if human presence were construed as belonging to man, rather than man being construed as belonging to human presence. To be sure, the notion that man belongs to human presence is a puzzling doctrine, but conceptually speaking, as I shall argue, there is much to be said for it.

The prime function of phenomena$_H$ in their interrelations, I hold, is a transcendental one: Being makes it possible for entities themselves to have functional (meaningful) status. The functions of Being, thus, enable entities to have functions in a derivative sense. This of course raises a number of difficult questions, most of which I listed at the end of the last chapter. What precisely is it that happens to entities by virtue of which they come to have functions? In what sense is human presence a set of functions? In what sense is it a happening? For entities to have functions what else, if anything, must happen to them beyond their being taken into a context of human agency and awareness? What is the precise relation of the functional status of entities to that which gives them this status? What are functions? How are they to be categorized? How do they relate to one another? And how do entities relate to the functions they possess?

In contrast to the more cautious piecemeal tendencies of the analytic tradition, which have resulted in a certain incompleteness in conceptual cartography, Heidegger presses toward a general doctrine of meaning. If the position I have adopted is correct, however, no general doctrine of meaning can be propounded prior to settling the ontological question concerning Being, regardless of which of the two interpretations of meaning, the *ing* or *ed* interpretation, one adopts. On the one hand meaning as Being disclosed cannot be comprehended apart from the Being of which it is a mode. On the other hand meaning as the disclosing of Being takes its character from Being insofar as Being is its "intentional" object. Thus the status of meaning is, to say the least, highly problematic.

Keeping in mind this problematic character and, more particularly, the dependence of meaning upon Being, let us consider how Heidegger relates language to meaning.

> That which can be articulated in interpretation, and thus even more primordially in discourse [intelligibility-articulation], is what we have called meaning. That which gets articulated as such in discursive articulation, we call the totality-of-significations [*Bedeutungsganze*]. This can be dissolved or broken up into significations. Significations, as what has been articulated from that which can be articulated, always carry meaning [. . . *sind . . . sinnhaft*]. . . . The totality-of-significations of intelligibility is *put into words*. To significations, words accrue. But word-things do not get supplied with significations.

> The way in which discourse [intelligibility-articulation] gets expressed is language. Language is a totality of words.[92]

Language is said to *express* meaning, though the manner in which it does this is left unspecified. Part of what is implied is that, through language, meaning quite literally gets *spoken out*. (The German verb is '*aussprechen*.') However, something much less innocent is implied also. Heidegger suggests a fairly sharp distinction between what gets expressed and the expressing of it. The former is given a definite independence of the latter. Meaning in the form of a totality-of-significations has a status of its own apart from language as a totality of words.

Heidegger's position is a relatively straightforward phenomenological position. Philosophically it is not as unorthodox as it might first appear to be. The failure of the phenomenologists to express themselves clearly on the matter has obscured this fact. Yet this doctrine is so basic to Heidegger, so pivotal to the development of

92. SZ g.161, e.204.

phenomenological philosophy as a whole, and so crucial to the reformulation of questions which concern me, that virtually no discussion of Heidegger, of phenomenology, or of the issues I have set
before myself can avoid a thorough investigation of it. It will be
helpful in this connection to examine some influential views of
Wittgenstein, comparing them at various points with those of
Heidegger.

In the *Philosophical Investigations*, section 15, Wittgenstein
writes concerning names and naming:

> The word 'to signify' is perhaps used in the most straightfor-
> ward way when the object signified is marked with the sign . . .
> It is in this and more or less similar ways that a name means
> and is given to a thing.—It will often prove useful in philos-
> ophy to say to ourselves: naming is like attaching a label to a
> thing.[93]

And again in section 26:

> To repeat—naming is something like attaching a label to a
> thing. One can say that this is preparatory to the use of a
> word.[94]

To be sure Wittgenstein understands naming to be but a prepara-
tion for the full-blown use of a word in language games. A word
may be used in a number of other ways than in its specific naming
or referring function:

> As if what we did next were given with the mere act of naming.
> As if there were only one thing called 'talking about a thing.'[95]

Yet naming is a language game in its own right:

> the processes of naming the stones and of repeating words after
> someone might also be called language games.[96]

    93. Ludwig Wittgenstein, *Philosophical Investigations*, trans. G. E. M.
Anscombe (New York, 1961), 7e. Hereafter cited as PI.
    94. PI 13e.
    95. PI (sec. 27).
    96. PI 5e (sec. 7).

For Wittgenstein the language game of naming involves things, utterances, and the process of labeling. Through labeling, utterances come to be associated with the things in such a way that the utterances become names, and the things are said to be labeled, attached with labels, or marked with signs. Labeling is a linguistic process by which utterances acquire meaning—though in a minimal sense—and things are marked in some manner. In this account of labeling priority is clearly given to language games by Wittgenstein.

Heidegger's explanation of labeling would be radically different. His view would require the substitution of the *Being* of entities for things, *intelligibility-articulation* for the process of labeling, and the *meaning* of the Being of entities, or perhaps just the totality-of-significations, for those same things as labeled or marked. Notice that the expressing of meaning or of the totality-of-significations in language would not be mentioned at all. In Heidegger's view such expression would presuppose that the labeling had already been accomplished. In this account of labeling, in contrast to Wittgenstein's, priority would clearly be withheld from language. Heidegger's view, which I endorse, would be this: entities are first articulated into their various functions and demarcated from one another—to use Wittgenstein's language they are first labeled—through Being itself progressively revealing itself in and through these entities. If, as I believe, 'λογος' is another expression for 'Being,' involved in labeling is nothing more nor less than Being making itself explicit. To the extent that Being makes itself explicit, entities are demarcated (functionally articulated) and thus made available in various ways for use by (human) agents. To say that Being makes itself explicit is to say at least this: in a prelinguistic way human presence becomes more aware of itself, a result of which is that entities within the world (world$_H$) of man are functionally articulated in more explicit ways and more explicitly distinguished from one another. Thus, on the surface at least the Heideggerian view is poles apart from Wittgenstein with regard to the place of language in the development of determinate awareness. But let us look a little more closely at Wittgenstein's account of naming. In particular, let us consider his views on ostensive teaching of words.

Wittgenstein holds that a child learns a language not by having it explained to him but by being trained in it:

The children are brought up to perform these actions, to use
these words as they do so, and to react in this way to the words
of others.[97]

The words to stress are 'perform,' 'use,' and 'react.' They indicate
that in the learning process language, which is experienced initially
by the learner as a natural (nonintentional) phenomenon, is fused
with activity. Through this fusion language takes on the characteristics of what Wittgenstein terms a language game. Such games are
for Wittgenstein intentional in nature and are the minimal cognitive or conceptual units in our experience. They are forms of behavior which he often refers to as "forms of life" (Lebensformen).
Much like other forms of behavior, a certain training is required
if the disposition to engage in them properly is to be inculcated. In
short, the ability to play a language game is a conceptual skill, and
training is viewed as the proper method of establishing such a skill.
To understand the words in a language game, which is necessary if
the learner is to play the language game, is to be able to *use* the
words, to *perform* certain activities in relation to them, and to *react*
to them appropriately.

> Don't you understand the call "Slab!" if you act upon it in
> such and such a way; . . . Doubtless the ostensive teaching
> helped to bring this about; but only together with a particular
> training. With different training the same ostensive teaching
> of these words would have affected a quite different under-
> standing.[98]

Ostensive teaching, as distinguished from training, is the act of
pointing to a particular object or aspect of an object and uttering
the name of that object or aspect. Training, on the other hand,
involves the total behavioral complex with which the ostensive
teaching is connected. The teaching is but one aspect of the total
behavioral complex. Training might include praise when the
learner becomes able to respond correctly to the words and to use
them correctly and punishment when his performance with the
words is inappropriate. For Wittgenstein, language games are

97. PI 4e (sec. 6).
98. PI 4e–5e (sec. 6).

learned primarily through this training. The emphasis is not on the ostensive teaching, for the ostensive teaching may be the same in two different situations, but the results may differ if the accompanying training differs.

Wittgenstein carefully distinguishes between ostensive teaching and ostensive definition. For an ostensive definition to do its job, the one for whom one defines the word must already be within the language game in which the word plays a role and must already have certain skills in playing that language game. Since training is the method by which the initial inculcation of these skills is accomplished, training is the means by which one first comes to language games. Given Wittgenstein's remark that

> what has to be accepted, the given, is . . . so one could say . . . *forms of life.*[99]

one must conclude that it is through training, linguistically oriented training in particular, that there comes to be something like a cognitive world of experience (something given in a cognitive sense). In short, training serves a transcendental function for Wittgenstein. Through training the learner makes the transition from nonintentional to intentional modes of behavior in any given domain.

One of the differences between the earlier and the later Wittgenstein is the account of how man comes to language. If one takes seriously the view that the possession of language defines man, this account is at the same time the account of man's coming into being. For the Tractarian Wittgenstein the transition from nonlinguistic and thus nonconceptual modes of behavior to linguistic-conceptual modes of behavior is holistic and in some sense instantaneous. Here we are speaking of the "hidden" language in the *Tractatus,* the mechanism of sense as it is sometimes called.[100] Wilfred Sellars presents the rationale for this position quite explicitly.

99. PI 226e.

100. See in this connection Richard Bernstein's "Wittgenstein's Three Languages," *Review of Metaphysics* 15 (December 1961) :278–98. The notion of a "mechanism of sense" I attribute to Robert Fogelin of Yale University.

I want to highlight from the very beginning what might be called the paradox of man's encounter with himself, the paradox consisting of the fact that man couldn't be man until he encountered himself. It is this paradox which supports the last stand of Special Creation. Its central theme is the idea that anything which can properly be called conceptual thinking can occur only within a framework of conceptual thinking in terms of which it can be criticized, supported, refuted, in short, evaluated. To be able to think is to be able to measure one's thoughts by standards of correctness, of relevance, of evidence: In this sense a diversified conceptual framework is a whole which, however sketchy, is prior to its parts, and cannot be construed as a coming together of parts which are already conceptual in character. The conclusion is difficult to avoid that the transition from preconceptual patterns of behaviour to conceptual thinking was a holistic one, a jump to a level of awareness which is irreducibly new, a jump which was the coming into being of man.[101]

For the later Wittgenstein the transition is clearly piecemeal and takes place over an extended period of time. Note his famous remark that

Our language can be seen as an ancient city: a maze of little streets and squares, of old and new houses, and of houses with additions from various periods; and this surrounded by a multitude of new boroughs with straight regular streets and uniform houses.[102]

I mention this presumed contrast between the two Wittgensteins as a means of suggesting Heidegger's view. Heidegger is a "Tractarian," though the sense in which this is the case requires some explanation. For human beings to be aware of anything at all, even of themselves, is for them to be aware of and to understand Being.[103] Naturally, to the degree to which Being is understood (disclosed), meaning is disclosed, for meaning is just Being itself

101. Sellars, *Science, Perception and Reality*, p. 6.
102. PI 8e (sec. 18).
103. SZ g.5, e.25.

insofar as Being can *be* disclosed. Thus an awareness and understanding of meaning, the meaning of Being, is the means by which
there first comes to be a cognitive world of experience—something
given in a cognitive sense.[104] It is the minimal cognitive, or conceptual, unit in our experience, and it is clearly holistic.[105] (Heidegger's term is 'equiprimordial,' which he predicates of the structures
of Being.) In other words, this minimal cognitive unit is not built
up in piecemeal fashion out of disparate parts.

Throughout *Being and Time* Heidegger insists that an awareness
of the meaning (functions) of Being is presupposed in all awareness of the meaning of Being's modes and characteristics.[106] This
holistic awareness and understanding thus serves the prime transcendental function for Heidegger. In Heidegger's view, which I
shall qualify later and then endorse, man cannot bring this transcendental condition into existence himself; insofar as man is defined in terms of a reflexivity which takes the form of self-awareness,
he himself first comes into being only *after* there is an awareness
and understanding of the meaning of Being. 'After' functions transcendentally rather than temporally. Reasoning in this way, Heidegger is prompted to make peculiar remarks. He says, for instance, that
Being is the happening that has man.[107] His meaning is that Being
happens to man in such a way as to bring man into being as man—
the being with an understanding of Being and through this understanding an awareness of entities, included among which is man
himself.

Let me add a parenthetical note. Though the line of reasoning
which leads Heidegger to these assertions is natural and insightful
if construed properly, it has dangerous implications. To say or
suggest that Being brings man into being is to border on anthro-
pomorphizing and reifying Being. That the concept of Being has a
transcendental priority over the concept of man need not lead one

104. In this connection, see SZ g.151 ff., e.192 ff.
105. SZ g.41, e.65, passim.
106. SZ g.37–38, e.61–62; g.8 ff., e.28 ff.
107. I am unable to locate the source of this quotation. I believe, however, that it occurs in *Identität und Differenz*. At any rate, the sense of the
doctrine should become clear from the considerations of chapter four.

to embrace a mystical or anthropomorphic view, however. I shall
have more to say about this later.

So far Heidegger would not have mentioned language (or for
that matter training). The comparison with Wittgenstein's *Tractatus* thus appears to be tenuous. Note, however, the sense in which
there is a holistic and instantaneous transition to language in the
Tractatus.[108] To do this we must reflect for a moment on the various languages mentioned, used, or suggested by this book.

A number of languages can be distinguished in the *Tractatus*.
There is, first of all, our everyday or ordinary language. Wittgenstein makes a number of remarks about it:

> everyday language is a part of the human organism and is no
> less complicated than it. . . . The tacit conventions on which
> the understanding of everyday language depends are enor-
> mously complicated. (4.002)

Further:

> all the propositions of our everyday language just as they stand,
> are in perfect logical order. (5.5563)

Yet:

> It is not humanly possible to gather immediately from . . .
> [everyday language] what the logic of language is. Language
> disguises thought. [Here presumably Wittgenstein is still
> talking about ordinary language.] So much so that from the
> outward form of the clothing it is impossible to infer the form
> of the thought beneath it, because the outward form of the
> clothing is not designed to reveal the form of the body, but
> for entirely different purposes. (4.002)

Quite clearly the transition to language in this sense is neither
holistic nor instantaneous. Everyday language is nothing more than
the complex of language games which is Wittgenstein's concern in
the *Investigations*. Presumably, therefore, it is learned in a succes-

---

108. Though Bernstein's article "Wittgenstein's Three Languages" does
not meet this point directly, his remarks are nonetheless instructive.

sive, piecemeal way. There is certainly no evidence to the contrary to be found in the *Tractatus*.

Beyond ordinary language there is, following Sellars, the "perspicuous" language.[109] This is an ideal language which is to be constructed in order to show perspicuously something that is hidden; it is the mechanism of sense, in other words the logico-conceptual process, the atomic propositions, by means of which language as it is actually used makes contact with the world as it is or can be presented. It is one of the main tasks of philosophy to construct such a language. The process of construction is, again, piecemeal and dependent for its development upon the discovery of truths in logic as well as in metaphysics—truths, for instance, concerning the status of properties, relations, and truth-functional connectives.

There is also the language used by Wittgenstein in the *Tractatus*, which is neither the everyday language nor the perspicuous language. This is a metalanguage for describing the perspicuous language, and most of the propositions of the *Tractatus* fall within its scope. But to have a metalanguage it is necessary first to have an object language, and thus the transition to language is not to be dealt with in the context of the metaphilosophical remarks which constitute the main body of the *Tractatus*.

The doctrine of the holistic transition to language, if it is to apply anywhere at all, must apply to the so-called "hidden" language in the *Tractatus*, the mechanism of sense. The mechanism of sense, however, is neither written nor spoken, since it is actually a language only in a very extended and metaphorical sense. Yet, it is not for that reason less basic to the linguistically oriented Wittgensteinian philosophy which sets the limits of the world at the limits of language. The mechanism of sense makes it possible for everyday language to make contact with the world, and it is expressed in disguised form in this language. It is also expressed in that perspicuous language that it is the philosopher's task to construct. The mechanism of sense thus resembles Heidegger's notion of intelligibility-articulation. For Heidegger, the transition to intelligibility-articulation is holistic, is expressed in "the most elemental words in

109. See again Bernstein's article. See also Sellars, *Science, Perception and Reality*, pp. 225 ff.

which Dasein expresses itself," and is to be expressed through the construction of an appropriate ontological grammar.

If the Tractarian conception of ordinary language is compatible with the doctrine of language games, then so is Heidegger's conception of language. For Heidegger, in fact, language takes the form of language games in its initial stages and insofar as it is a "living" language.[110] A totality-of-significations, Heidegger claims, precedes the significations into which it is subsequently analyzable. This totality is not to be built up out of separate items.[111] Since language rests upon this totality and derives its character from it, it cannot itself be construed to be a conjunction of separately functioning units which come together in external fashion to constitute actual speech. Rather, language must be understood to be a whole of parts—as a living language, *wholes* of parts—in which the whole has some normative and thus prior status with respect to the parts. There is one particular passage in *Being and Time* which well illustrates the close connection between language and the Wittgensteinian notion of language games. After having stated that assertion is a derivative mode of interpretation, Heidegger says that:

> we can point out the modification if we stick to certain limiting cases of assertion which function in logic as normal cases and as examples of the "simplest" assertion-phenomena. Prior to all analysis, logic has already understood "logically" what it takes as a theme under the heading of the categorical statement—for instance, 'the hammer is heavy.' The unexplained presupposition is that the "meaning" of this sentence is to be taken as: This thing—a hammer—has the property of heaviness. In concernful circumspection there are no such assertions "at first." But such circumspection has of course its specific ways of interpreting, and these, as compared with the "theoretical judgment" just mentioned, may take some such form as 'The hammer is too heavy,' or rather just 'Too heavy!,' 'Hand me the other hammer!' Interpretation is carried out primordially not in a theoretical statement but in an action of cir-

110. This obviously is more interpretive than expository. In this connection, see SZ g.160 ff., e.203 ff.

111. SZ g.161, e.204.

cumspective concern—laying aside the unsuitable tool or exchanging it, "without wasting words." From the fact that words are absent, it may not be concluded that interpretation is absent. On the other hand, the kind of interpretation which is circumspectively *expressed* is not necessarily already an assertion in the sense we have defined. . . . Between the kind of interpretation which is still wholly wrapped up in concernful understanding and the extreme opposite case of a theoretical assertion about something present-at-hand, there are many intermediate gradations: assertions about the happenings in the environment, accounts of the ready-to-hand reports on the situation, the recording and fixing of the "facts of the case," the description of a state of affairs, the narration of something that has befallen. We cannot trace back these "sentences" to theoretical statements without essentially perverting their meaning. Like the theoretical statements themselves, they have their "source" in circumspective interpretation.[112]

Let us return now to our discussion of the learning of language games in the *Philosophical Investigations,* for if there is a striking similarity between the Tractarian Wittgenstein and Heidegger with regard to the status of language, there is as striking a similarity between Heidegger and the later Wittgenstein with regard to language games.

Ostensive definition, if it is to be effective, presupposes that the one for whom one defines the word is already within the language game in which the word plays a role and already has certain skills in playing that language game.

So one might say: the ostensive definition explains the use—the meaning—of the word when the over-all role of the word in language is clear. . . . One has already to know (or be able to do) something in order to be capable of asking a thing's name.[113]

Take for example the case of color words: 'red,' 'blue,' 'green,' and so on. By pointing to various colors and in connection with a certain

112. SZ g.157–58, e.200–01.
113. PI 14e–15e (sec. 30).

training it is possible to develop in the learner the skill of being able to use color words. Through training the learner comes to know his way about in the "logical space" which color words occupy. He can then be said to understand the role played by color words.

But this is not all. When training in the skill is accomplished the learner may himself ask about colors whose names he does not have. For Wittgenstein, the learner is now open to the world of color itself, whereas before the linguistic training he was not. Having had the limits of his language expanded, the learner's world is expanded too. It is intelligible to him in a new dimension. In short, its intelligibility has been articulated for him in ways which go beyond, for a time at least, the scope of the words he possesses for expressing its articulated distinctions. A gap exists between the colors the learner is able to discriminate and the words he possesses for making the discriminations. As more and more names of colors are learned, the articulated intelligibility of the world of color gets *expressed* for him in language.

Given this account, Heidegger's appeal to phenomena_H in the form of prelinguistic structures is similar even to the later views of Wittgenstein. For Heidegger the colors the learner had become able to discriminate would be phenomena in the ordinary sense of the term. That by means of which this discrimination became possible—for Wittgenstein the logical or conceptual space of color to which the learner is brought through training; for Heidegger, intelligibility-articulation—would be phenomena_H, structures of Being. These structures as articulated would constitute a subdomain of the meaning (functions) of Being. The names of the colors and their grammar would be the language by means of which the phenomena and phenomena_H get *expressed,* and through an analysis of this language the phenomena and phenomena_H get revealed. For both Heidegger and Wittgenstein meaning thus transcends, in some contexts at least, language as language is ordinarily understood; yet it comes to be expressed in language.

Among the many differences between Heidegger and Wittgenstein there are perhaps two major ones. Heidegger would claim that meaning—the meaning of Being, roughly equivalent to the sum of the various logical or conceptual spaces suggested by the *Philosoph-*

ical Investigations—has a univocal pan-transcendentality which ranges in nongeneric fashion over all language games and the forms of life (worlds of experience) which they adumbrate. He conceives it his task to bring this transcendentality to expression through the forging of a language grammatically equipped to deal with the conceptual difficulties and peculiar cartographical problems presented by the meaning of Being. Secondly, Heidegger thinks that man is brought into the realm of meaning (explicit functions) not through training but rather by means of the presence of Being itself —in short, that the transition to peculiarly human modes of behavior must remain a mystery.[114] Note finally, however, that Wittgenstein no less than Heidegger fails to present a theory or doctrine concerning the nature of meaning and how meaning is experienced by human beings. Thus both leave the status of language in a highly problematic state; both accounts of the relation of language to meaning are difficult to construe. As I have tried to point out, however, there are definite similarities of a positive sort between the two philosophies and these should not be obscured by the more obvious differences.

With regard to the concept of meaning, Wittgenstein and Heidegger are typical of the traditions they represent. Questions concerning the relation of language to meaning, thus, are answered unsatisfactorily by both of the major schools of contemporary philosophical thought. The primary reason for this is that the proper questions are not asked. In both traditions, though in the linguistic tradition only covertly, meaning is held to have a prelinguistic status. This view I believe correct. I construe meaning, minimally at least, as a context of human awareness and agency, of human presence, *prelinguistic in nature,* which functions in various ways in relation to entities. These functions cause entities themselves to have functional status and to modify this status at times. It is clear that this view drives a wedge between language and some dimensions of meaning and raises difficult problems concerning their reunion. The verbs 'reflect,' 'express,' and 'articulate' do little to overcome these problems. The concept of isomorphism does less.

114. This is perhaps the most unpalatable of Heidegger's doctrines. It comes out particularly in his later writings.

What is the precise relation of language to prelinguistic meaning? The view of meaning I have presented forces this question, though neither of the major traditions has posed it with great enough care or with sufficient appreciation of its importance. For phenomenologists the "expression" of meaning in language is a mysterious happening. For analytic philosophers it does not receive official recognition as a problem. Yet no other account of meaning than the one I have presented does justice to a number of facts. Consider a few of the more obvious ones. With changes in human attitudes and concerns, some changes in the quality and structure of human experience occur. The advent of romanticism represented such a change, as did the development of the therapeutic dimension of contemporary psychiatric theories. Whether modifications in the pattern of human experience are cause, effect, or neither is of no concern. In any case, in periods of transition people, individually and in groups, find themselves having to grope for words to describe their new experiences. Old metaphors die, and new ones come to take their place. Some phrases are found to be appropriate, others inappropriate. This distinction cuts across the distinction between old and new uses of words, old and new words. In periods of transition people judge the appropriateness of expressions in terms of the accuracy of those expressions with respect to the experiences they are used to describe. In short, experience itself, prior to its linguistic appropriation, serves as a linguistically mute criterion for its own description. If meaning were not in some respects antecedent to language, this obvious fact could not be. Modifications in human experience would be incomprehensible, and their description would be a curious blend of convention and caprice. If meaning were not in some respects antecedent to language, the labors of a number of contemporary poets, scientists, and novelists would be equally incomprehensible.

What enables language to "express" prelinguistic meaning? Does language necessarily fall short of full articulation of this meaning? Are there respects in which language conceals prelinguistic meaning? In what ways do linguistic and prelinguistic meanings relate? To what extent is the language which "expresses" prelinguistic meaning composed of words? Can such a language have other constituent elements, as Wittgenstein suggests when he says in his *Zettel:*

> Understanding a musical phrase may also be called understanding a *language.*[115]

These questions, answers to which are crucial to the assessment of the philosophical significance of language, concern the relation of language to the totality of phenomena_H in their interrelations. In short, they concern the role of language in the phenomenological method.

I turn now to a brief consideration of some linguistic methods and devices, particularly nonetymological ones, employed by Heidegger in the service of phenomenology. The most important of these is Heidegger's reliance on *existential* uses of words. For Heidegger, the term 'in,' for instance, functions most straightforwardly and in the most philosophically perspicuous way in statements such as

> John is *in* philosophy.

or

> George is *in* trouble.

or

> Ralph is *in* love.

It functions not only less clearly but often misleadingly in statements such as:

> The book is *in* the drawer.
> The table is *in* the room.
> The conference room is *in* Building Five.

Heidegger holds that existential uses of words are paradigmatic. Other uses are extended and sometimes metaphorical, but always more abstract applications of the terms.[116]

115. Wittgenstein, *Zettel*, trans. G. E. M. Anscombe (Oxford, 1967), 30e (sec. 172).

116. See SZ g.221, e.262; g.53 ff., e.79 ff.

The consequences of an unequivocal reliance on this view are peculiar. Presumably a clear understanding of, for example, space and the spatial dimensions of the human world (world$_H$) is best gained through a careful study of statements such as these:

> They were never close to each other.
> Keep in touch.
> He's lost contact with himself.
> He was beside himself with grief.
> She was feeling low.
> He had no room in his life for others.
> She was rather shallow, but his thoughts were deep.

Now it is not uncommon for philosophers to speak in somewhat the following way: the use of spatial terms in philosophical discourse concerning such things as the mind is admissible, provided that one realizes the metaphorical import of the terms in such contexts. As both a historical and philosophical fact, however, the metaphors have seldom been recognized for what they are, or, if they have, their significance as metaphors usually has not been comprehended. On the whole, therefore, the use of spatial metaphors has exerted a pernicious influence in philosophy, particularly in the philosophy of mind. Such metaphors are best avoided in philosophical writing, for they are inexact, and though the question concerning the nature of space is not a particularly difficult or for that matter philosophical question, the question concerning spatial metaphors and their import and conceptual rationale is most difficult and frustratingly philosophical.

This line of thought is totally out of touch with the spirit of Heidegger's philosophy and in this regard, it seems to me, Heidegger is correct. All questions concerning space are at least partially philosophical. To understand space one must analyze the concept of space as an ingredient in one's discourse and experience. This I take to be a minimal and justifiable Kantian requirement. The requirement does not go far enough, however. One must also describe space as it is experienced prelinguistically. Space must be described with respect to those of its features which form part of the conceptual structure of one's world$_H$. If the conceptual behavior of spatial terms is to be clarified and understood, all sophisticated theoretical notions of space must thus in the end be related back to this experiential context of meaning, this transcendentally fundamental locus of human presence, which in large measure is prelinguistic. The proper articulation of this context (the functions of Being in their interconnection) is philosophy's major business. To relate a theoretical framework back to an observational or experiential framework, however, is not to reduce the former to the latter. The phenomenological notion of *grounding* carries no such commitment.[117]

What follows from an espousal of this strategy is the relegation of more theoretical notions of space to secondary status. They should be viewed as abstract, perhaps even metaphorical, extensions of the concept of space. Even the statement

> The chair is *close* to the window.

must be understood to be an exemplar of a relatively abstract understanding of space—compared, for instance, to a statement such as

> They are close friends.

In short, existential uses of spatial notions must be taken to be fundamental in a transcendental sense. Their uses are most perspicuous in the adumbration of the fundamental structures of human presence. To come to know the nature of space as we actually experience it and as our language articulates it requires a careful exploration of the conceptual cartography of "existential spatiality." All other uses of spatial terms and all other experiences of space are founded upon this base.

There are two other nonetymological uses of language which I wish to mention briefly. Heidegger takes garden-variety sayings very seriously.[118] Take as an example the concept of time. Some of the most "elemental words" in which man expresses himself concerning time are these:

117. This, of course, is at variance with Wild's interpretation. See Wild, *Existence and the World of Freedom,* pp. 80 ff.
118. SZ g.220, e.262 is where the programmatic commitment to this procedure is found.

I have no time for him.
Time goes fast when you're enjoying your work.
I've little time.
Time seemed to stand still.

For Heidegger, whose view I believe correct, these would adumbrate time as we actually experience it. Statements such as these give access to primordial time, which philosophy must describe.

I understand primordial time as time insofar as it has status as a phenomenon$_H$ and, thus, constitutes in part the locus of human agency and awareness. The time statements I have offered present the philosopher with the raw materials out of which is to be developed the set of concepts required for a genuinely explicit and philosophical comprehension of time. I base this claim on the same transcendental grounds offered in defense of the significance of existential uses of terms.

In his later writings Heidegger appeals to poetic language.[119] He thinks insights are to be gained from a sensitive analysis of the work of certain poets whose careful use and abuse of language reveal clearly the qualities and structures of various primordial human experiences.[120] Though indispensable to the existence and history of man, these experiences are for the most part left linguistically unappropriated.[121] Some poets, Heidegger thinks, forge language by means of which to recapture these experiences or to capture for the first time new experiences of fundamental significance.[122] This view of the importance of poetic language is insightful. Poetic language is of a piece with existential uses of terms and folk sayings in this regard. It reveals features of human agency and awareness which are basic to the continued existence of man as we know him or could conceive of him on the basis of what we do know. In short, poetic language often reveals perspicu-

119. See in this connection n. 76, above.

120. See in this connection Heidegger, "Remembrance of the Poet," and "Hölderlin and the Essence of Poetry," trans. Douglas Scott, in Existence and Being, ed. Werner Brock (Chicago, 1949), pp. 233–91.

121. Ibid. See also SZ g.21 ff., e.43 ff.

122. See n. 120, above.

ously prelinguistic meaning, the phenomena$_H$ of phenomenology, and thus bears witness to human presence and its structure and functional propensities as they develop over time. Of the results of careful etymological analysis I would argue the same.

I have now endorsed a number of uses of language in the service of phenomenology. My endorsements, all of which rest on transcendental grounds, depend for their defense upon a certain view of the significance of phenomenology and a certain philosophical position on the nature of human worlds. I shall turn to man and his world in the last chapter. Here I would like to point out that the chief value of phenomenology lies in its recognition of the gap that exists between linguistic and prelinguistic meaning. This enables it to take human history seriously and thus to construe philosophical anthropology as perhaps *the* central philosophical discipline. Human history is in large measure the history of the relation of the expressed to the unexpressed, of the linguistic to the prelinguistic. This history constitutes the history of man himself. Recognizing the meaning gap, as I shall term it, phenomenology is able thus to concern itself thematically with important questions about language, its power, history, and limits. These questions can be asked within the broad context of human agency and awareness, an unalterable prerequisite of methodological self-consciousness. Insofar as phenomenology construes meaning in a broad and partially prelinguistic sense, its comprehension of the proper subject matter of philosophy—meaning—conforms more closely to that subject matter itself. To be sure, linguistic phenomenology, the careful description and classification of the conceptual behavior of terms as they function in various language games, is an important dimension of phenomenology. But it is only a dimension. In recognizing a prelinguistic human world which language seeks to appropriate, phenomenology opens itself to various aspects of human experience that are basic to the fabric of human presence. Since Freud it has been seen that practical action and the language that surrounds it are not necessarily fundamental with respect to the mechanisms of human agency and awareness. To reach the basic dimensions is to reach something transcendentally fundamental, which is at the heart of human presence. These basic dimensions are adumbrated by phenomenology and can be reached, in part at least, through a careful examination of the uses of language I have just considered.

The term 'language' and its variants recur at crucial points in what I have said. What is the philosophical significance of language? This question I now wish to reformulate. I offer in its stead a number of questions, some of which I have already mentioned in the course of this chapter. How does language relate to prelinguistic meaning, both conceptually and historically? What significance is to be found in the fact that languages have histories? What sense does it make to speak of the "predispositions" of a given language with respect to the articulation of prelinguistic meaning? Given that there are such predispositions, do they differ from one language to another? Precisely what features of language and which of its uses enable it to "express" prelinguistic meaning? What are the limits, if any, of language's ability to articulate this meaning? Are there respects in which language conceals this meaning? How does language relate to the meanings it possesses? In short, what precisely is *linguistic* meaning? Is it necessary that the language which "expresses" prelinguistic meaning be composed of words? Can such a language have other constituent elements?

There are three other questions I wish to list. The first two presuppose certain answers to some of the earlier questions. The last gives indication of problems yet to be confronted. What is the conceptual behavior and interrelation of prepositions in their existential uses? What interpretation of language offers a perspicuous explanation of the phenomenological significance of folk sayings, poetry, and etymology? In what way does language belong to man and man to language?

The last question points to a set of problems which the other questions all presuppose. As is true with discussions of the concept of meaning, any discussion of language must remain incomplete until there has been a careful analysis, in part transcendental, of the being who makes use of language: man. It is to some of the thorny issues surrounding the concept of man, in particular to the concept of human world, that I now turn.

CHAPTER 4

The Doctrine of Mediated Reflexivity

Our primary concern has been with two items: Being, which I have identified with meaning, and language. I have offered two major theses concerning their conceptual geography: the interrelated structures (functions) of Being constitute the transcendental phenomena of phenomenology. And certain features of language provide the means of access to these phenomena. In this chapter I turn to a selective consideration of Heidegger's views on man (Dasein) and, through this consideration, to a reformulation of the third guiding question: What is a (human) world?

Being for Heidegger is always the Being of an entity. His goal is to analyze the nongeneric meaning of Being as such, taking into account the differences in the Beings of the particular entities to which it "happens." In *Being and Time,* however, Heidegger examines the Being of just one entity, man. The importance of considering Heidegger's account of the Being of this entity resides in a curious set of facts. In philosophical taxonomy Heidegger is usually classified not as a philosopher of Being, but as an existentialist. This is virtually always the case when Heidegger is judged in terms of his actual philosophical accomplishment. To be sure, there is an existential dimension to Heidegger's work, but its function is not in any classical sense existential. If this is not seen, Heidegger is seriously misunderstood and the problems I wish to clarify through him, cannot properly be reached. I begin this chapter, therefore, with a set of twenty-one theses which both interpret the significance of Heidegger's putative existentialism and explain why an analysis of Being quickly turns into an analysis of human being in *Being and Time.* The theses are difficult but extremely important. They present a consistent, highly condensed argument that reveals the major connections between Heidegger's most important concepts. After this synopsis I return to comment and elaborate upon some of the relatively abstract points involved. In the course of the discussion two matters will be of major concern: the transcendental role of the concept of world, and the status of Being in relation to man. First, however, the synopsis of Heidegger's position, which I preface with a definition:[1]

Definition: Dasein is the entity which each of us himself is.[2]

(1) Dasein's Being is its existence *(Existenz)*.[3]

(2) Dasein's existence is that of which it is aware in being aware of itself.[4]

(3) That of which Dasein is aware in being aware of itself is its understanding-of-being *(Seinsverständnis)*.[5]

(4) Dasein's Being is its understanding-of-Being.

(5) Questioning is a mode—that is to say, one of the functions—of Dasein's Being.[6]

(6) Questioning is one of the functions of Dasein's understanding-of-Being.

(7) In particular, the questioning-of-Being—the putting of the question of the meaning (functions) of Being —is one of the functions of the understanding-of-Being. In Heidegger's parlance, the *Seinsfrage* is a mode of the *Seinsverständnis*.[7]

1. What follows is a sustained argument which, I believe, shows Heidegger's position in its basic structural features. The definition I offer is not verbatim from Heidegger, nor is the argument itself.

2. SZ g.41–42, e.67–68.

3. SZ g.42, e.67.

4. This follows transcendentally. If awareness of any *x* requires an awareness of the Being of that *x*, then for Dasein to be aware of itself is for it to be aware of its existence.

5. SZ g.5–6, e.24–25. This thesis is in a way the fundamental thesis of *Sein und Zeit*. It is made explicit nowhere and yet used everywhere. See also SZ g.34 ff., e.58 ff.

6. In this connection, see EIM g.14–16, e.15–17; g.22–23, e.24–25. See also SZ g.212 ff., e.256 ff.; g.295 ff., e.341 ff. These passages are not conclusive but offer strong evidence for the thesis.

7. See in this connection the passages cited in the previous footnote.

(8) To understand the questioning-of-Being is to understand the understanding-of-Being, of which the questioning-of-Being is one of the functions.

(9) The questioning-of-Being is the authentic mode (the prime function) of the understanding-of-Being.[8] Thus the understanding-of-Being which Dasein is and always possesses, as Dasein, must be made authentic—that is to say, it must be intensified or radicalized—if the question of Being is to be asked. In fact, to make the understanding-of-Being authentic is nothing more and nothing less than to put the question of the functions of Being.[9]

(10) Since the understanding-of-Being is Dasein's Being, to make Dasein authentic is to put the question of the functions of Being.

(11) The understanding-of-Being is structured in such a way that in part at least it takes its understanding of Being as such, and thus indirectly its understanding of itself, from its understanding of the Being of entities other than Dasein.[10] Being is always the Being of an entity. Thus the understanding of Being as such must proceed by means of an understanding of some entity in its Being. When the entity through which the understanding-of-Being gets its understanding of Being as such is an entity other than Dasein, that understanding-of-Being is said to be inauthentic *(uneigentlich)*.[11] Dasein's Being therefore is so structured that it is at least in part inauthentic. The understanding-of-Being tends to construe the structures constitutive of the Being of entities other than Dasein as applicable in some primary sense to Being as such. These structures are termed cate-

8. See especially SZ g.295 ff., e.341 ff.

9. I take this to be the underlying motive of Heidegger in analyzing the phenomenon of conscience.

10. SZ g.44, e.70; g.179 ff., e.223 ff., and passim.

11. For a discussion of the concept of inauthenticity, see SZ g.41–44, e.67–70.

gories.[12] The indirect result is that the understanding-of-Being construes these same structures as belonging to itself.[13]

(12) In the light of this, Heidegger's program in *Being and Time* is to "authenticate" (bring to authenticity) the awareness of that of which Dasein is aware in being aware of itself—in short, to authenticate Dasein's awareness of its understanding-of-Being.[14] Since part of what is included in the understanding-of-Being is the understanding of the Being of Dasein, an authenticating of the *awareness* of the understanding-of-Being is an authenticating of the understanding-of-Being itself. It is an authenticating of the Being of Dasein.

(13) The authenticating of Dasein's awareness of its understanding-of-Being will put Dasein in a position to disclose the structures of its understanding-of-Being.[15] These structures are termed existentials *(existentialia)* as opposed to categories.[16] Once disclosed, the existentials are to serve as clues to the nature of Being as such and thus, at least indirectly, as clues to the nature of the Being of entities other than Dasein.[17]

(14) These existentials are referred to as the context of existentiality, which is roughly parallel with Kant's table of categories.[18] The task of discovering this context is the business of an existential analytic or, alternatively, of fundamental ontology.[19] It is an exist*ential* undertaking.[20]

12. SZ g.44–45, e.70–71.
13. SZ g.41 ff., e.67 ff. This is clearly a matter of interpretation. Later sections of SZ bear it out however. See, for instance, g.89 ff., e.122 ff.
14. SZ g.231–35, e.274–78.
15. Ibid.
16. SZ g.41 ff., e.67 ff.
17. In this connection, see SZ g.8 ff., e.28 ff.
18. SZ g.12–13, e.33.
19. SZ g.12 ff., e.33 ff.
20. Ibid.

(15) An authenticating of Dasein's awareness of its understanding-of-Being is not identical with and need not
issue in the performance of an existential analytic.
Becoming authentic does not entail that one do fundamental ontology. This may neither be aimed at nor
conceived to be possible. The notion of an understanding-of-Being may not be comprehended at all.
If this happens, the undertaking has little philosophical import. It is but an exercise in existentialism.
Existentialism is an existent*iell* rather than an existent*ial* enterprise.[21]

(16) An existent*iell* undertaking need not result in fundamental ontology, but it is a necessary prerequisite of
such an ontology.[22] It is in this sense and this sense
alone that Heidegger is an existentialist.

(17) Dasein's Being has an important reflexive characteristic: as an understanding of Being as such and in its
various modes, the understanding-of-Being includes
as part of what it understands an understanding of
itself, for the understanding-of-Being is the Being of
entities of the nature of Dasein and thus one of
Being's modes. This reflexive element in the understanding-of-Being is its crucial element. Heidegger
refers to it as Dasein's disclosedness *(Erschlossen-
heit)*.[23] Authenticated reflexivity is referred to as
resoluteness *(Entschlossenheit)*.[24]

(18) More particularly, Heidegger's program in *Being
and Time* is to show how Dasein's understanding-of-
Being can be authenticated (brought to resoluteness).
To be resolute is to put the question of the functions
of Being, however unthematically.[25] In fact, to put

21. See in this connection SZ g.12, e.33; g.338 f., e.387 f.
22. SZ g.267 ff., e.312; g.305 ff., e.352 ff.
23. SZ g.133, e.171.
24. SZ g.296–97, e.343.
25. In this connection, see EIM g.15–17, e.16–18. See also SZ g.267 ff.,
e.312 ff.

this question is equivalent to being resolved. Dasein is to be brought to resoluteness so that it can perform an existential analytic.

(19) *Being and Time,* thus, is a reflection on the reflexive character of Dasein's Being for the purpose of intensifying this reflexivity into resoluteness. The penultimate goal of this reflection is a philosophical interpretation of the structures (existentials) constitutive of intensified reflexivity. The ultimate goal is a philosophical interpretation of the meaning of Being as such in all its modes—in other words, a philosophical articulation of the totality of Being's functions in their interrelations.

(20) Existentials are constitutive of both an authentic and an inauthentic understanding-of-Being. They are more accessible, however, to an authentic understanding-of-Being.[26] Existentials are equiprimordial *(gleichursprünglich).*[27] Though they are intimately interrelated, they cannot be fitted into a hypothetico-deductive system.

(21) The design of *Being and Time* was the following: Part One: the interpretation of Dasein in terms of temporality, and the explication of time as the transcendental horizon for the question of Being. Part Two: basic features of a phenomenological destruction of the history of ontology, with the problematic of temporality as our clue. Part One has three divisions:

1. The preparatory fundamental analysis of Dasein;
2. Dasein and temporality;
3. time and Being.

Part Two likewise has three divisions:

1. Kant's doctrine of schematism and time, as a

26. SZ g.231–34, e.274–77.
27. SZ g.191, e.235, and passim.

preliminary stage in a problematic of temporality;

2. the ontological foundation of Descartes' *"cogito sum,"* and how the medieval ontology has been taken over into the problematic of the *"res cogitans;"*

3. Aristotle's essay on time, as providing a way of discriminating the phenomenal basis and the limits of ancient ontology.[28]

The first division of the first of the two projected parts of *Being and Time* articulates those existentials which are revealed on the basis of an inauthentic understanding-of-Being.[29] The second division of this first part articulates those further equiprimordial structures which are revealed on the basis of an authentic understanding-of-Being and allows for a more insightful grasp of the existentials revealed in the first division.[30] None of the other projected divisons or parts of *Being and Time* has appeared in print.

Without a clear picture of what Heidegger means by the term 'Dasein,' these relatively abstract theses cannot be seen for what they are: metaphenomenological *descriptions* of what goes on when the descriptive business of phenomenology is carried out properly. This brings us to a consideration of the significance of the term 'Dasein' for Heidegger and to an examination of some of the particular features which Heidegger ascribes to the entity denoted by this term. Heidegger's pivotal remarks on the topic are peculiar:

The entity which is essentially constituted by Being-in-the-world *is* itself in every case its "there." According to the familiar signification of the word, the "there" points to a "here" and a "yonder." The "here" of an "I-here" is always understood in relation to a "yonder" ready-to-hand, in the

28. SZ g.39–40, e.63–64.

29. This clearly is a matter of interpretation. In this connection see SZ g.41 ff., e.67 ff.; g.231 ff., e.274 ff.

30. See the preceding footnote.

sense of a Being towards this "yonder" ... The "yonder" belongs definitely to something encountered within-the-*world*. "Here" and "yonder" are possible only in a "there"—that is to say, only if there is an entity which has made a disclosure of spatiality as the Being of the "there." This entity carries in its ownmost Being the character of not being closed off. In the expression 'there' we have in view this essential disclosedness. By reason of this disclosedness, this entity (Dasein), together with the Being-there *(Da-sein)* of the world, is "there for itself." When we talk in an ontically figurative way of the *lumen naturale* in man, we have in mind nothing other than the existential-ontological structure of this entity, that it *is* in such a way as to be its "there." To say that it is "illuminated" [*erleuchtet*] means that *as* Being-in-the-world it is cleared [*gelichtet*] in itself, not through any other entity, but in such a way that it *is* itself the clearing. . . . By its very nature, Dasein brings its "there" along with it. If it lacks its "there," it is not factically the entity which is essentially Dasein; indeed, it is not this entity at all. *Dasein is its disclosedness.*

We are to set forth the constitution of this Being. But in so far as the essence of this entity is existence, the existential proposition, 'Dasein is its disclosedness,' means at the same time that the Being which is an issue for this entity in its very Being is to be its "there."[31]

The crucial characteristic of Dasein is its reflexivity, its relatedness to itself. In Dasein this reflexivity is found in non–totally reflexive form in the phenomenon of self-awareness. It is the reflexive features of Dasein's self-awareness that give Dasein its unique philosophical significance. With regard to self-awareness Heidegger is in alliance with Kant and the Husserlian phenomenological tradition, standing thus in direct opposition to the influential, neo-idealistic views of Descartes and the school of French Reflexive Analysis.[32] Self-awareness for Heidegger is always me-

31. SZ g.132–33, e.171.

32. See in this connection Pierre Thévenaz, *What is Phenomenology? And Other Essays,* ed. James M. Edie, trans. Charles Courtney, and Paul Brockelman (Chicago, 1962), pp. 113 ff.

diated:[33] one cannot be aware of oneself without at the same time being aware of something other than oneself. Alternatively, whenever one is aware of oneself, one is aware of oneself as standing in relation to something else. Note that both of these formulations are but restatements in less mentalistic and more wholesale terms of the classical phenomenological doctrine of intentionality—the doctrine that consciousness is always consciousness of, that it always *intends* (directs itself towards), an object which it distinguishes from itself. Kant states this doctrine first. He does so somewhat obliquely however, for he is very much the victim of the representationalist distinction between the "inner" and the "outer." In the second edition of his *Critique of Pure Reason* in the short section entitled "Refutation of Idealism" Kant writes:

> even our inner experience, which for Descartes is indubitable, is possible only on the assumption of outer experience . . . In other words, the consciousness of my existence is at the same time an immediate consciousness of the existence of other things outside me. . . . inner experience is itself possible only mediately, and only through outer experience.[34]

Kant's "outer experience" is the experience of Newtonian nature. This experience is made possible, Kant thinks, by the categories of the understanding operating under the limitations imposed by the pure forms of sensibility. For Kant it is only because one is able to experience Newtonian nature that one can experience oneself. To use Heidegger's terms, this is the ontic dimension of Kant's doctrine of mediated self-awareness. One can in turn experience Newtonian nature, Kant thinks, only because

> [one is] in possession of certain modes of *a priori* [synthetic] knowledge [*gewisser Erkenntnisse a priori*], and even the common understanding is never without them.[35]

A priori synthetic knowledge for Kant is transcendental knowledge. The "object" of transcendental knowledge is the subject's

---

33. SZ g.132–33, e.171, and passim.
34. KdRv g.273–75, e.244–46 (B275–77).
35. KdRv g.39, e.43 (B3).

contribution to experience. By means of this contribution, Kant claims, experience assumes a cognitive dimension. Strictly speaking, the "object" of transcendental knowledge is *not* an object however; rather, it is that set of necessary conditions which makes a world of experience cognitively possible. For Kant it is only because one is able to experience cognitively this set of conditions that one can experience Newtonian nature and thus ultimately oneself. To use Heidegger's terms again, this is the ontological dimension of Kant's doctrine of mediated self-awareness. In *Kant and the Problem of Metaphysics* Heidegger writes:

> Kant means: not "all knowledge" is ontic, and where such knowledge is given, it is possible only through ontological knowledge,[36]

and, again:

> What makes the relation to the essent (ontic knowledge) possible is the precursory comprehension of the constitution of the Being of the essent, namely, ontological knowledge.[37]

Heidegger thinks that self-awareness is mediated by something ontically more concrete than Newtonian nature and ontologically more basic than the categories and pure forms of sensibility of Kant's critical philosophy. To work this out both ontically and ontologically is to undercut Kant's philosophy. More particularly it is to reveal and to describe things as they are in themselves, entities within one's world as well as the totality of phenomena$_H$ (functions of Being) which make experience of these entities possible. Heidegger thinks himself in a position thus to exploit Kant's critical doctrines by a tour de force.

Let us return to the term 'Dasein.' 'Dasein' for Heidegger denotes those interrelated, equiprimordial elements which constitute mediated self-awareness.[38] Here a distinction must be made between one's actual, empirical awareness of oneself on the one hand and the structures which make this empirical awareness possible on

36. KB g.22, e.17.
37. KB g.20, e.15.
38. SZ g.132–33, e.171.

the other. Self-awareness in its empirical actuality is the ontic dimension of Dasein. In other words, it is Dasein as a being or entity. As an ontic term 'Dasein' is roughly equivalent to 'empirical apperception' *(empirische Apperzeption)* in the Kantian philosophy. Mediated self-awareness in its structural possibility constitutes the ontological dimension of Dasein. It constitutes Dasein's understanding-of-Being. Dasein's understanding-of-Being is roughly parallel in the Kantian philosophy with transcendental apperception *(transcendentale Apperzeption),* the original synthetic unity of apperception.

When Heidegger states that

> [Dasein] *is* in such a way as to be its "there,"

he suggests with the term 'there' both the "self" and "other" aspects of mediated self-awareness and their inextricable interrelation. The term 'there' is one of the chief means he uses to indicate Dasein's mediated reflexivity and thus Dasein itself. His initial remark concerning it is linguistic:

> According to the familiar signification of the word, the "there" points to a "here" and a "yonder."

Consider first the ontic realm. That which, in being "yonder" (other), serves the basic mediating function in self-awareness is by no means entities understood in terms of the conceptual framework of Newtonian nature. Heidegger explicitly rejects in ontological terms this view of the entities encountered within one's world:

> If one understands Nature ontologico-categorially, one finds that Nature is a limiting case of the Being of possible entities within-the-world.[39]

Rather, and again in ontological terms:

> The Being of those entities which we encounter as closest to us can be exhibited phenomenologically if we take as our clue our everyday Being-in-the-world, which we also call our

39. SZ g.65, e.93–94.

"dealings" in the world and *with* entities within-the-world. Such dealings have already dispersed themselves into manifold ways of concern. The kind of dealing which is closest to us is . . . not a bare perceptual cognition, but rather that kind of concern which manipulates things and puts them to use; and this has its own kind of "knowledge." The phenomenological question applies in the first instance to the Being of those entities which we encounter in such concern. . . . in our dealings we come across equipment for writing, sewing, working, transportation, measurement.[40]

Heidegger claims that, with the exception of one's own and other Daseins, the entities encountered within one's world have as their mode of Being (their function) either "presence-at-hand" *(Vorhandenheit)* or "readiness-to-hand" *(Zuhandenheit).*[41] He construes presence-at-hand as the Being of entities when they are revealed as (Newtonian) nature[42] and readiness-to-hand as the Being of entities when they are comprehended as equipment.[43] Parallel with the ontic priority of equipment over nature in Heidegger's thought, readiness-to-hand is given ontological priority over presence-at-hand.[44] Thus that which serves the *ontological* mediating function in self-awareness for Heidegger is Being itself, understood primarily in its mode of readiness-to-hand.

Heidegger draws a relatively sharp distinction between his position and that of the tradition. Heidegger makes the claim that previous philosophy has concerned itself with a conceptual account of entities solely in their presence-at-hand.[45] Thus on his view the entities within one's world have not been properly understood by previous philosophers. Since self-awareness is mediated ontically by an awareness of the entities within one's world and ontologically by an awareness of the Being of these entities, a philosophical mis-

40. SZ g.66–68, e.95–97.
41. SZ g.66 ff., e.95 ff.
42. SZ g.74, e.104; g.202 ff., e.246 ff.
43. SZ g.66 ff., e.95 ff.
44. SZ g.89 ff., e.122 ff.
45. SZ g.21–22, e.43–44.

understanding of the entities within one's world and particularly of their Being has resulted in a philosophical misunderstanding of self-awareness and thus of the "self" as well. It is this state of affairs that Heidegger sets out to correct.

More needs to be said about the distinction between readiness-to-hand and presence-at-hand as modes of Being and about equipment and nature as ways of characterizing entities. Some account is also needed of how these distinctions arise for Heidegger. All of these matters are bound up with what amounts to a transcendental deduction in Heidegger's thought. The deduction grows out of his conception of the "there." Unfortunately not all of its steps are clear.

Heidegger understands the "there" (mediated reflexivity) to be made up of three basic components. One of them is intelligibility-articulation *(Rede)*. Heidegger terms the other two components 'state-of-mind' *(Befindlichkeit)* and 'understanding' *(Verstehen)*.[46] That intelligibility-articulation should be viewed as a constitutive factor in mediated reflexivity is not hard to understand. The doctrine of mediated reflexivity states that for one to be aware of oneself is for one to be aware at the same time of something other than oneself. This formulation presupposes that in a suitably broad sense one can be brought into or find oneself in the presence of something other than oneself. For Heidegger, intelligibility-articulation serves precisely this function. Intelligibility-articulation is understood to be the making manifest or bringing out into the open of what is to be "discussed"—which is to say, of what is to be fixed in language and thereby made the object of explicit cognitive apprehension—in such a way that everything that comes to be said about it is drawn from it itself. In accordance with the doctrine of mediated reflexivity it is, in part at least, intelligibility-articulation that allows one to be in the presence of oneself. Since reflexivity in the form of self-awareness is taken by Heidegger to be a (perhaps even *the*) constitutive factor of man as man, it is in part at least through intelligibility-articulation that man comes to be man.

I turn now to a consideration of state-of-mind *(Befindlichkeit)*.

46. SZ g.142 ff., e.182 ff.; g.134 ff., e.172 ff.

As we saw, it is Heidegger's view that for one to experience something *as* something, one must experience that something *in terms
of* one's world$_H$.[47] One's world$_H$ serves as a necessary condition for
the possibility of one's experience. This doctrine has an important
corollary: with one exception all knowledge is mediated. Given
any *x*, one comes to know that *x in terms of* one's world$_H$. One's
world$_H$ thus serves a mediating function. The exception to the
doctrine is in regard to knowledge of one's world$_H$ itself. One cannot know it in terms of something other than itself. It must be
comprehended in terms of itself—which is to say that knowledge
of one's world$_H$ must be immediate rather than mediated. For
Heidegger one's state-of-mind—more particularly, one's mood
(Stimmung) taken as a particular state-of-mind—is the primary
source of this immediate knowledge:

> As we have said earlier, the world which has already been
> disclosed beforehand permits what is within-the-world to be
> encountered. This prior disclosedness of the world belongs to
> Being-in and is partly constituted by one's state-of-mind. . . .
> Indeed *from the ontological point of view* we must as a gen-
> eral principle leave the primary discovery of the world to
> "bare mood."[48]

Heidegger assigns two other functions to moods as well. The
first is connected with Heideggerian notion of "thrownness"
(Geworfenheit).[49] One's mood is said to reveal to one the fact *that*
one is and that one can be no one other than oneself. This revelation, it is said, yields no knowledge of one's origin or destiny as a
human being. Heidegger thinks that this deficiency in the revelation is essential to it as a revelation of "thrownness."

> In having a mood, Dasein is always disclosed mood-wise as
> that entity to which it has been delivered over in its Being;
> and in this way it has been delivered over to the Being, which,
> in existing, it has to be. "To be disclosed" does not mean "to

47. See pp. 88 ff.
48. SZ g.137–38, e.176–77.
49. SZ g.135, e.174.

be known as this sort of thing." And even in the most in-
different and inoffensive everydayness the Being of Dasein
can burst forth as a naked "that it is and has to be." The pure
"that it is" shows itself, but the "whence" and the "whither"
remain in darkness. . . . the Being of the "there" is disclosed
moodwise in its "that-it-is" . . . This characteristic of Dasein's
Being—this "that it is"—is veiled in its "whence" and
"whither," yet disclosed in itself all the more unveiledly; we
call it the "thrownness" of this entity into its "there," indeed,
it is thrown in such a way that, as Being-in-the-world it is the
"there."[50]

What Heidegger has in mind is difficult to express in appropriate
words, though the experience is not altogether uncommon. Some
of it is undoubtedly captured by Albert Camus in *L'Étranger*.[51] One
need not look to prose fiction or poetry, however, to get a sense
of what is meant. At some time or other probably everyone has
become acutely aware of himself—not with regard to particular
personal characteristics or peculiar features of a situation in which
he finds himself, but simply in the fact that he exists. Though it
usually involves some feeling of uncanniness, perhaps accompanied
by feelings of despair or elation, the experience is not particularly
mystical. Some psychiatrists in fact urge the cultivation of the experience as a means of fostering psychic health.[52] In the experience one is simply aware of oneself as existing. Together with this,
one is confronted with the elusively obvious: one has no choice
but to be oneself and to make of oneself what one can, given the
limitations that being oneself imposes. To deny mystical status
to the experience is to deny to the experiencer any special knowledge through the experience. Through the experience one gains
no insight into the reasons, if any, for one's having been brought
into being. Neither does one glimpse the fate which is to befall
one.

50. SZ g. 134 ff., e.173 ff. See especially g.134–36, e.173–75.
51. See in this connection "Hölderlin and the Essence of Poetry," in
Existence and Being, pp. 270–91.
52. See in this connection Erich Fromm, *The Art of Loving* (New York,
1956), pp. 107 ff.

One's moods are also said to reveal one's "Being-in-the-world" as a whole. This point is closely tied in Heidegger's account to his conception of the locus and status of moods.

> From what has been said we can see already that a state-of-mind is very remote from anything like coming across a psychical condition by the kind of apprehending which first turns round and then back. Indeed it is so far from this, that only because the "there" has already been disclosed in a state-of-mind can immanent reflection come across "experiences" at all. The "bare mood" discloses the "there" more primordially, but correspondingly it *closes* it *off* more stubbornly than any *not*-perceiving.
>
> This is shown by *bad moods*. In these Dasein becomes blind to itself, the environment with which it is concerned veils itself, the circumspection of concern gets led astray. States-of-mind are so far from being reflected upon, that precisely what they do is to assail Dasein in its unreflecting devotion to . . . [those entities within the world] with which it is concerned and on which it expends itself. A mood assails us. It comes neither from "outside" nor from "inside," but arises out of Being-in-the-world, as a way of such Being. But with the negative distinction between state-of-mind and the reflective apprehending of something "within," we have thus reached a positive insight into their character as disclosure. *The mood has already disclosed, in every case, Being-in-the-world as a whole, and makes it possible first of all to direct oneself towards something.* Having a mood is not related to the psychical in the first instance, and is not itself an inner condition which then reaches forth in an enigmatical way and puts its mark on things and persons.[53]

'Being-in-the-world' *(In-der-Welt-Sein)* is used by Heidegger to indicate a fundamental structure of Dasein.[54] In accordance with the doctrine of mediated reflexivity, Dasein's awareness of itself

53. SZ g.136–37, e.175–76.
54. SZ g.41, e.65; g.52 ff., e.78 ff.

includes an awareness of something other than itself. The term 'there,' Heidegger believes, captures this fact. Heidegger holds that 'Being-in-the-world' performs the same function. Dasein's Being is "in the world" in the sense that Dasein always finds itself enmeshed in a world of concern. It not only finds itself enmeshed in such a world, it comes to distinguish itself from other objects of its concern *in terms of* that world of concern. Only in this way does it become itself explicitly *as* self-awareness. Thus Heidegger can say that

> *mood has already disclosed, in every case, Being-in-the-world as a whole, and makes it possible first of all to direct oneself towards something.*

This account of 'Being-in-the-world' ties in closely with Heidegger's conception of Being itself. When Being happens to Dasein what results is mediated reflexivity: the conferral upon Dasein of both self- and other-awareness. Being thus brings Dasein into being as Dasein. Since in the Kantian transcendental sense all awareness presupposes an awareness of Being, the bringing about of Dasein as Dasein is thus simultaneously, though more basically in the order of transcendental priorities, the creation of an awareness of Being. That there is an awareness of Being, however, is as essential to Being, Heidegger holds, as it is to Dasein.[55] In a sense, therefore, the bringing about of Dasein is at the same time the bringing about of Being itself:

> Entities *are,* quite independently of the experience by which they are disclosed, the acquaintance in which they are discovered, and the grasping in which their nature is ascertained. But Being "is" [*ist*] only in the understanding of those entities to whose Being something like an understanding of Being belongs. Hence Being can be something unconceptualized, but it never completely fails to be understood.[56]

Of course only as long as Dasein is (that is, only as long as an understanding of Being is ontically possible) "is there" [*gibt*

---

55. In this connection, see Richardson, *Heidegger.*
56. SZ g.183, e.228.

es] Being. When Dasein does not exist . . . it cannot be said that entities are, nor can it be said that they are not. . . . As we have noted, Being (not entities) is dependent upon the understanding of Being.[57]

As the translators of *Being and Time* point out, the German phrase *'gibt es'* (in English, 'there is') is problematic in the second of these passages. In an attempt to discourage a misguided interpretation of his thought, Heidegger claims in his letter *Über den Humanismus*[58] that the phrase must be taken literally:

for the "it" which here "gives" is Being itself. The 'gives,' however, designates the essence of Being, which gives and which confers its truth.[59]

Since it is of the essence of Being to give itself, and Being can give itself only to Dasein, Heidegger's special interpretation of the *'es gibt'* phrase leaves his major point untouched: that there is an awareness of Being which is as essential to Being as it is to Dasein. For this reason Dasein sustains a quite special relation to Being: Dasein and Being are in "mutual need" of each other.[60] In *Being and Time* the problems involved in working out an account of this peculiar relationship are neither solved nor clarified. Heidegger is only concerned to describe the understanding-of-Being and to show how this understanding can be modified so as to bring about an adequate comprehension of Being. I shall return to this relationship near the end of this chapter, clarify it, and endorse some conceptual points that follow from my clarification.

In revealing mediated reflexivity in the fact that it is—a transcendental revelation which is at the same time one's encounter with oneself in the fact that one is—and in revealing mediated reflexivity in its structure as that in terms of which experience

---

57. SZ g.212, e.255.

58. This essay is reprinted in *Platons Lehre von der Wahrheit* (Bern, 1947). It also appears separately as *Über den Humanismus* (Frankfurt a.M., n.d.).

59. Heidegger, *Über den Humanismus*, p. 22.

60. Richardson discusses this relationship extensively in *Heidegger*.

assumes a cognitive dimension, moods play a central function in Heidegger's thought. Heidegger's views on this function are not altogether unambiguous, however. In *Being and Time* moods are said to reveal one's world$_H$, a constitutive element of mediated reflexivity and therefore a structure of one's Being. So long as one's world$_H$ can be viewed as a structure of one's Being, this doctrine is not only compatible with the other statements Heidegger makes about moods, it complements them by stressing one of their most important implications: the task moods have of revealing Dasein's Being. Soon after the writing of *Being and Time*, however, Heidegger presents a slightly different account of the role of moods, and at roughly the same time the world$_H$ begins to lose its status as a component element of Dasein's Being and takes on characteristics previously ascribed solely to Being itself.[61] These two developments are not unconnected. I want to repeat the suggestion that, for Heidegger, world$_H$ comes to be identified with Being itself. This identification requires that world$_H$ gain a certain independence of Dasein's Being. Granting this independence, a peculiar consequence follows if one continues to hold the view that one's moods reveal one's world$_H$. Moods can no longer be construed as revealing Dasein's Being alone. Rather, they must be understood to reveal Being itself too. They thus become ambiguous in their function. Heidegger's thought bears out this ambiguity.[62]

Consider his post–*Being and Time* position with respect to the function of moods. In his inaugural address upon having acceded to the chair of philosophy at the University of Freiburg, Heidegger examines one particular mood, anxiety *(Angst)*.[63] In *Being and Time* anxiety is understood to be Dasein's most fundamental mood. Through it Dasein is brought to its most primordial encounter with itself in the fact that it (Dasein) is. This particular means of self-encounter reveals to Dasein at the same time Dasein's Being-

61. See in this connection Heidegger, "What is Metaphysics?" trans. R. F. C. Hull and Alan Crick, in *Existence and Being*, pp. 325–61. I shall refer to this essay simply as "What is Metaphysics?" in subsequent footnotes.

62. This, of course, depends upon the juxtaposition of *Being and Time* with "What is Metaphysics?"

63. The address is published as "What is Metaphysics?" See n. 61 above.

in-the-world as a whole and its world$_H$.[64] In his inaugural address, however, Heidegger assigns to anxiety a different function. Here its primary task is to reveal "the Nothing" *(das Nichts)*. This "Nothing" is later identified with Being itself.[65] It now becomes Being itself rather than simply Dasein's Being that anxiety most fundamentally reveals.

To be sure, it is possible to hold that anxiety reveals *both* Dasein's Being *and* Being itself. Since Dasein's Being is its under-standing-of-Being, and Being "is" only in and for an understanding-of-Being, Being and Dasein's Being cannot be revealed apart from each other. The revelation of an understanding-of-Being is at the same time the revelation of the Being understood, a consequence of the doctrine of intentionality, and the disclosure of Being is simultaneously a disclosure of the understanding-of-Being, a con-sequence of Heidegger's phenomenological development of the epistemological implications of Kant's central critico-transcendental thesis. The emphasis, however, is now placed on Being, while in *Being and Time* it was placed on Dasein's Being.

Though Heidegger's claim that moods come neither from within nor from without may appear to contradict rather obvious facts, the point *is* "phenomenological." In Heidegger's view it cannot in the strict sense be phenomenological, for it has to do with entities, and properly speaking phenomenology deals solely with Being. Often, however, the term 'phenomenological' is used honorifically by phenomenologists as a synonym for 'descriptive,' a fact which makes possible the designation of a large number of linguistic analysts as "linguistic phenomenologists." Given this understanding of phenomenology, Heidegger's point clearly *is* phenomenological. It is a plausible description of moods. No scandal is involved in asserting the freedom of moods from the predicates 'inner' and 'outer' if one remains faithful to one's experience and the language in which that experience is usually described. It makes linguistic sense, for instance, to say:

64. SZ g.184 ff., e.228 ff.
65. See Heidegger, "What is Metaphysics?" pp. 325–61.

I am in the mood for some entertainment.
He is in a very foul mood.
She could not get out of that mood all evening.

But it would be odd to say:

The mood for some entertainment is in me.
A very foul mood is in him.
She could not get that mood out of her all evening.

One need not appeal exclusively to linguistic usage to establish the inappropriateness from the descriptive standpoint of ascribing interiority to moods. It is the world of one's concern, a world which includes one's person as one of its elements, that gets characterized in terms of mood's predicates, not some process or psychic state within one. Moods are not in me. I fall into *them.* When I do, they color the entire situation in which I find myself. Thus Wittgenstein can say with no small insight that:

The world of the happy man is a different one from that of the unhappy man.[66]

Moods are no more susceptible to the interpretation that they come from without. It makes sense to say:

He put them into a good mood.
She fell into a bad mood.
I got into a reflective mood and lapsed into silence.

But it would not be altogether coherent to ask questions concerning the location of moods with respect to one's person prior to or after one's having gotten, fallen, or been put into them. Moods neither come from nor go anywhere, though they are at times infectious. The infectiousness, however, cannot be explained in terms of the predicational devices of the inner and the outer. In short, whatever properties moods may have, spatial properties are not among them.

These linguistic and phenomenological observations are but reflections on the "logic" of mood situations. Heidegger obviously

66. *Tractatus* 6.43.

takes such situations seriously and after reflecting upon them assigns to moods the basic functions we have just discussed. How do moods perform the various tasks he allots to them however? What are the mechanisms which enable them to perform their revelatory functions? Heidegger's answer to these questions is unhelpful:

> one does not know. And Dasein cannot know anything of the sort because the possibilities of disclosure which belong to cognition reach far too short a way compared with the primordial disclosure belonging to moods, in which Dasein is brought before its Being as "there."[67]

> As a matter of fact, Dasein can, should, and must, through knowledge and will, become master of its moods; in certain possible ways of existing, this may signify a priority of volition and cognition. Only we must not be misled by this into denying that ontologically mood is a primordial kind of Being for Dasein, in which Dasein is disclosed to itself *prior* to all cognition and volition, and beyond their range of disclosure.[68]

Here Heidegger expresses the conviction, shared by Wittgenstein and the phenomenological tradition,[69] that a philosophical account of cognitive mechanisms is bound to be arbitrary. The philosopher who best exemplifies this mistaken philosophical approach is Kant.[70] In the first edition of the *Critique of Pure Reason,* particularly in the A deduction, Kant speaks of necessary conditions for the possibility of experience. He says that experience is only intelligible after a certain stage is reached in the organization of its data; nonetheless, Kant offers an account of how this stage is attained, an account of what "faculties" are involved and what procedures they employ. As other philosophers have pointed out, this

67. SZ g.134, e.173.
68. SZ g.136, e.175.
69. In general these philosophers reject the tendencies toward a priori psychology and "constructivism" inherent in so much philosophy. See, for example, P. F. Strawson, *The Bounds of Sense, An Essay on Kant's Critique of Pure Reason* (New York, 1966).
70. Clearly this is the force of the A deduction. In this connection, see Strawson, *The Bounds of Sense,* pp. 15 ff., 85 ff., and passim.

account is, on Kant's own terms, both epistemologically and metaphysically specious. Kant's philosophy does not permit such remarks to be made. The "positivistic" side of phenomenology can be seen in its insistence that philosophy confine itself to experience, a manifesto which is in the spirit of the transcendental implications of Kant's philosophy.

Heidegger's position is that the furthest cognitive penetration possible by means of moods is their revelation of the fact of one's mediated reflexivity. This they reveal as the "in terms of which" of mediated cognition and thus as one's world$_H$. To speculate on the means by which moods accomplish their functions is simply to speculate, which is not to do phenomenology. This last point has its parallel in Wittgenstein's remarks about reading.[71] A description of reading is a philosophical task. An explanation of the mechanisms involved in reading, when offered by philosophers, is an exercise in the philosophy of mind in its marginal, pseudoscientific dimensions. Much the same sort of comments could be made about the philosophical study of moods. For the idealistically oriented German tradition, such work in the philosophy of mind tends to be viewed as metaphysics itself and its scope is construed to extend, as in Hegel, even to the natural world.[72] Phenomenology represents an important departure from this tradition.

It is not difficult to see the manner in which intelligibility-articulation and mood (state-of-mind) relate as coconstitutive components of mediated reflexivity. The doctrine of mediated reflexivity requires awareness of something other than self if there is to be awareness of self. This requires in turn that in a relatively broad sense one can be brought into or find oneself in the presence of something other than oneself, a task performed in part by intelligibility-articulation (λογος). Much like Kant's categories of the understanding, it is through the λογος that entities are experienced in their determinate Being. Intelligibility-articulation thus is the principal factor involved in bringing about the awareness of something other to oneself, for awareness as cognitive must in every

71. PI 61e ff. (secs. 156 ff).

72. One might read Hegel's philosophy, in fact, as a near reductio ad absurdum of this philosophical program.

case be determinate, and it is the λογος that brings about this determination.

Though intelligibility-articulation is the principal factor involved in awareness of something as other, it is not the sole factor. For one to be aware of anything whatsoever one must be aware of it in terms of one's Being-in-the-world as a whole. In short, awareness of any entity presupposes awareness of one's world$_H$ as that in terms of which entities are experienced. Mood performs this vital function, and thus it is as indispensable as intelligibility-articulation in the constitution of mediated reflexivity. Since reflexivity in the form of self-awareness is taken by Heidegger to be the prime constitutive component of man as man, it is in part through the interrelated functions of intelligibility-articulation and mood that man comes to be as man. I say "in part" for we have yet to discuss the third constituent of mediated reflexivity: understanding. In many ways this component is the most important one:

> State-of-mind is *one* of the existential structures in which the Being of the "there" maintains itself. Equiprimordial with it in constituting this Being is *understanding*. A state-of-mind always has its understanding, even if it merely keeps it suppressed. Understanding always has its mood.[73]

That no mood is without its understanding is a puzzling doctrine. One's mood reveals one's Being, which is mediated reflexivity. Heidegger has still another term by which he refers to this mediated reflexivity. It is sometimes designated as one's situation *(Situation)*.[74] Although the term has certain advantages, it can be misleading, since it entails the truth of the statement that one *is* one's situation. One's situation, after all, is simply one's awareness of oneself as bound up in circumstances, and the latter phrase is but another way of expressing the doctrine of mediated reflexivity. In no case however should this position be confused with classical doctrines of existentialism. When the existential philosophers claim that man is his situation or that he "is" what he "does," they have something more voluntaristic in mind than does Heidegger,

73. SZ g.142–43, e.182.
74. SZ g.299, e.346.

and they mean by 'situation' something which is more empirically determinate.[75]

To comprehend the role of understanding *(Verstehen)* in Heidegger's thought is to realize that the "circumstances" in which one mediately finds oneself are not merely a function of "objective" factors. Rather, they are a function of these factors seen in terms of the possibilities they offer for one's action and the threats they pose to this action. These possibilities and threats in turn are a function of what one conceives one's basic possibilities of action to be. In short, they are a function of one's fundamental purposes.

The point Heidegger wishes to make is subtle and somewhat elusive. It has definite connections with certain pragmatic doctrines and an even more intimate relation to some views held by Nietzsche and recent linguistic analysts. An illustration drawn from the realm of common experience will serve to clarify what Heidegger has in mind. Consider a person standing in a room. What is the best way to characterize his circumstances? One might say, for instance, things of the following sort:

> He is approximately twenty-five feet from the only door leading out of the room.
>
> He is approximately twenty-one feet from someone who plans to reproach him if given the chance.
>
> The would-be reproacher stands near a piano.
>
> The piano is only six feet from the door.
>
> There are seven other people between him and the man who wishes to reproach him.

One could characterize these circumstances in more detail, or more abstractly, or in both ways at once. Reference could be made to a three-dimensional spatial region within which certain objects are located at certain distances from one another and from an arbitrarily chosen point. These objects could be characterized as having certain properties, and so on. Whether expressed more or less ab-

75. This, at any rate, has been the usual interpretation of Sartre's views, particularly as found in his literary writings.

stractly, the basic elements in this account would be objects having properties and standing in various relations to one another in a space which is, roughly speaking, Newtonian.

Heidegger would allow that the circumstances *could* be characterized in this way. He would argue however that such a characterization would be superficial as a description of the actual experience of the person whose circumstances these are. For Heidegger a more genuine description of the circumstances would involve statements like the following:

> The person in question is far enough from the door so that if he tries to reach it directly he will be observed by his would-be reproacher.

> He is close enough to the seven men between himself and the reproacher so that he could walk up to them without being noticed by the reproacher.

> The seven men are so close to the piano that if he walks up to them he has a good chance of slipping behind the piano and out the door without being noticed at all by the reproacher.

In Heidegger's view what is directly experienced are determinate circumstances.[76] These circumstances are experienced in terms of the possibilities they open to human beings in their roles as agents. One's circumstances are not only constituted by these possibilities, they are said to be these possibilities.

> "Being towards" a possibility—that is to say, towards something possible—may signify "Being out for" something possible, as in concerning ourselves with its actualization. Such possibilities are constantly encountered in the field of what is ready-to-hand and present-at-hand—what is attainable, controllable, practicable, and the like. In concernfully Being out for something possible, there is a tendency to *annihilate the possibility* of the possible by making it available to us. But the concernful actualization of equipment which is ready-to-hand (as in producing it, getting it ready,

76. SZ g.66 ff., e.95 ff.

readjusting it, and so on) is always merely relative, since even that which has been actualized is still characterized in terms of some involvements—indeed this is precisely what characterizes its Being. Even though actualized, it remains, as actual, something possible for doing something; it is characterized by an "in-order-to."[77]

Circumstances are constituted as particular possibilities because of the fundamental possibilities or purposes of an agent. The agent not only *has* these possibilities or purposes, in some sense he *is* them.

Dasein is not something present-at-hand which possesses its competence for something by way of an extra; it is primarily Being-possible. Dasein is in every case what it can be and in the way in which it is its possibility. . . . possibility as an *existentiale* is the most primordial and ultimate positive way in which Dasein is characterized ontologically.[78]

In the example just given it is the purpose of avoiding the notice of the would-be reproacher that constitutes the circumstances as a particular set of determinate possibilities. Were some other purpose motivating the agent, the circumstances would be understood in a different way.

Clearly there are a number of objections one could raise against this account. The major objection is perhaps the following: contrary to Heidegger's view, circumstances as they are in themselves are *given* in the technical philosophical sense of the term. The various possibilities for human action which these circumstances *offer*, rather than *are*, are added to them through the presence of human agents. Distinguishing the residual given from the added elements, the objection continues, is not an insuperable task. The progress of science requires that the distinction be made successfully, and the advance of technology depends upon its reasoned exploitation.

I believe this objection to be unsound. If part of the business of

77. See in this connection SZ g.261, e.305.
78. SZ g.143–44, e.183.

philosophy is to describe human experience, Heidegger's point is
well taken. Undeniably we do experience entities in terms of their
usefulness to our purposes. Not only this, such experience is primary. The experience of entities apart from their potentialities for
human use and threats to human purpose is at best derivative. It is
a luxury of dubious value to experience entities as function-free.
To deny the primacy of "practical" experience—given Kant's transcendental doctrines transmuted into theses concerning language—
is to reinstate the Tractarian view of language, its structure and
function, in the face of Wittgenstein's rather devastating critique
of this position in his *Philosophical Investigations*.[79] Words do
not function primarily to denote objects any more than objects
appear to us primarily in isolation from other objects and from the
purposes of human agents which give them their character. First
and foremost objects, like words, are experienced as functionally
interrelated to serve practical ends.

One might argue that the question is not what is first in the order
of experience. It is what is most perspicuous as an analysis of experience. Surely, this argument would continue, the most objective
and fruitful analysis of experience, even from the standpoint of its
exploitation for further human use, involves the distinction between the given and those increments added by human agents.
There are three replies to be made to a critic who argues in this
manner. First, if experience is to be described—if, as Wittgenstein
and others suggest, the business of philosophy is essentially descriptive[80]—there is no denying the centrality to philosophy of
the core structure of experience. This core is clearly purpose-ori-
ented and it takes a great deal of effort to reorient oneself to experience one's world in any other way. Perhaps such reorientation
is impossible. Second, any analysis of experience must find in its
ultimate constituents the means by which to reconstitute experience as it is initially given. Though associationalist doctrines in
philosophical psychology have long since been discredited, the
view that human beings, through their associations with objects,

79. See in particular the sections on Language Games and Logic. PI 31e ff.
(secs. 65 ff.), 42e ff. (secs. 89 ff.).
80. PI 50e (sec. 126).

add pragmatic features (practical values) to those objects has had a longer life. The test of the doctrine is whether, by means of its categories, experience can be reconstituted once it has been dissected into preexisting objects and various inner states of percipient organisms. I do not think that it can, though a negative thesis of this sort resists convincing proof. The closest to verification one can come is to point out that no plausible reconstruction of experience in these terms exists, save perhaps in the form of promissory-note-laden scientific programs. The third point I wish to make concerns the notion of an entity existing independently of human agency and awareness, definable without reference to human purpose, and explicable without recourse to functional relationships, active or passive, sustained to other entities. The existence of an entity of this sort I do not wish to deny, though I refrain from asserting its existence as well. What concerns me is the concept of such an entity. It seems to me that within this concept is the concept of purpose. The purpose in this case is to describe entities in isolation from other entities perhaps and certainly from human concerns. Is this purpose self-referentially consistent? Can the purpose of describing without reference to purpose avoid commitment to the concept of purpose? Can a type distinction save the essentially purpose-free commitment of the concept of a "pure" description or explanation? The answer to these questions must be negative. Describing entities in their putative functionless state, their "presense-at-hand," is not altogether possible. Such a description, much like Wittgenstein's conception of the hidden language in the *Tractatus,* is an ideal, suited to some things but not to others. It is purpose-laden, though the purposes are more theoretical than practical. It serves interests in intellectual symmetry, cohesion, and organization rather than overtly pragmatic, everyday interests. The purpose of dealing with entities in their presence-at-hand is certainly not the most common or frequent way of dealing with them. Rather, it is an abstraction from the everyday concerns of human agents. Why should it, any more than the concept of an ideal language, function normatively with respect to experience, especially if its account of experience does not and cannot account for entities as actually experienced?

If the concept of purpose, which is synonymous with the concept of function, is essential to the concept of an entity, a curious line of reasoning gains considerable plausibility.[81] For one to be aware of something other than oneself, the argument runs, is for one to be aware of it in its usefulness, actual or potential. It is one's own purposes, however, that articulate entities other than oneself into their functional characteristics. It is in terms of one's own purposes, thus, that entities become amenable to the only possible cognitive interpretation of them, which is a functional one. To have purposes of one's own, however, is to be aware of oneself, and one is aware of oneself only mediately, only insofar as one is aware of entities other than oneself. Here we are confronted with a circle. How do we break out of it? Heidegger claims that it is through understanding. For Heidegger, the understanding projects a basic function (purpose) for the self. In terms of this function the self becomes aware of itself. At the same time this function articulates a set of concepts in terms of which entities other than the self are comprehended in their functional character.[82] In a basic transcendental sense, thus, the understanding's projective act constitutes one's situation. In short, it constitutes mediated reflexivity, man as man, for the concept of awareness presupposes the concept of agency, and the understanding makes possible this concept and the functional concepts it entails.

From a conceptual standpoint the act of understanding clearly is not something which a man can be said to perform. For a man to do something he must first be an agent. His agency, however, presupposes the successful performance of the act of understanding. Thus in some sense this act must precede man. It constitutes a world in terms of which experience can be interpreted. In doing this it brings man into being. Note again the close connection between this set of doctrines and the views of Wilfred Sellars, who presents roughly the same thesis in slightly different language.

The "manifest" image of man-in-the-world can be characterized in two ways, which are supplementary rather than

---

81. See in this connection nn. 77–78 above. See also SZ g.263–64, e.308–09.

82. SZ g.66 ff., e.95 ff.; g.142 ff., e.182 ff. See also g.235 ff., e.279 ff.

alternative. It is, first, the framework in terms of which man came to be aware of himself as man-in-the-world. It is the framework in terms of which, to use an existentialist turn of phrase, man first encountered himself—which is, of course, when he came to be man. For it is no merely incidental feature of man that he has a conception of himself as man-in-the-world, just as it is obvious, on reflection, that if man had a radically different conception of himself he would be a radically different kind of man.[83]

Heidegger and Sellars both suggest (though Sellars ultimately denies) the irreducible, holistic, and, with respect to the nonintentional, discontinuous character of intentional modes of behavior. Man cannot be the source of the intentional, for the concept of man presupposes the intentional. Thus, in a sense which requires further analysis, intentionality precedes man.

These doctrines force one to confront a difficult set of alternatives. One might hold to a continuity thesis, arguing, as Sellars does, the reducibility of the intentional to nonintentional[84] status. Here, however, one faces all the conceptual difficulties involved in the translation of intentional statements into nonintentional ones. These difficulties have not been solved. To my knowledge no philosopher has claimed to solve them. The reducibility thesis is curiously Hegelian. One is forced to speak utopianly of what the various postulational sciences, particularly quantum mechanics, will eventually achieve. To make philosophy the handmaiden of a not yet existent science, a phantom science, is a dangerous mistake. It replaces the empiricism of philosophy with metaphysical speculation cloaking itself in the respectable garb of natural science. If the conceptual problems remain unsolved—and are perhaps in principle unsolvable—the reducibility thesis has no philosophical value.

A second alternative is held by Peirce. Intentionality is viewed as irreducible, but capable of piecemeal development and ultimate absorption of the nonintentional. To hold this position is to claim

83. Sellars, *Science, Perception and Reality*, p. 6.
84. Ibid.

that there was no time before which intentional modes of behavior failed to exist.[85] One can speak of the gradual development of more complex modes of intentionality, but never of the advent of the intentional. This position has a great deal to be said for it. It shares with the philosophy of Merleau-Ponty an important insight into the distinction between a rule and a regularity. A rule is something in accordance with which intentional activity is guided. Through appeal to rules predictions and explanations are possible on conceptual grounds. A regularity on the other hand is something in accordance with which nonintentional activity is described. It it not presumed that regularities explain anything, and the predictions they yield are viewed merely as statistical probabilities which assume the uniformity of nature and depend for their accuracy upon nothing more than mathematical calculation. Laws, even those in the natural sciences, because normative, are rules and thus indicate behavior which in an important sense is intentional.[86] The nominalist and positivist accounts of the significance of the natural sciences consistently miss this point. A further advantage of Peirce's view concerns the relation between man and other forms of life. Peirce is better able to construe the elements of continuity in this relation because he has removed intentionality from exclusive residence in the domain of human consciousness. In this respect his view accords more closely with experience. Holding to Peirce's view, however, one is still forced to resort to myth or the concept of chance to explain the development of those symbolic modes of intentionality which we identify as peculiarly human. This is the major drawback to Peirce's position. The obvious elements of discontinuity between human and other forms of consciousness are only obscured when the concept of continuity is used to explain the development of intentional modes of behavior. Discontinuity as well as continuity requires explanation. For the former Peirce's position is inadequate, if only in that it is incom-

85. Peirce, *Collected Papers of Charles Sanders Peirce I & II,* ed. Charles H. Hartshorne and Paul W. Weiss (Cambridge, 1960), pp. 141 ff. and passim.

86. Ibid., pp. 197 ff. and passim. In this connection, see Merleau-Ponty, *La Structure du Comportement* (Paris, 1942).

plete as an account of the flowering of the various products of human consciousness.

The last alternative is Heidegger's, namely, that in a transcendental sense Being takes precedence over man.[87] This position I believe correct. The grounds for this endorsement are three. First, it is a conceptual truth that man presupposes the intentional and thus cannot be its source. Second, an explanation of intentional modes of behavior by appeal to the continuity of their development fails to account for the gap which exists between human and other forms of intentional activity. Third, even if one holds Peirce's view, the Heideggerian position with respect to the individual man remains valid. If only in the form of communal rules, linguistic and nonlinguistic, the structures of the intentional have a transcendental priority over incoming members, individual humans developing full human consciousness in terms of those rules. This may be to impute more credibility to Peirce's (and Wittgenstein's)[88] position than it deserves, however. If one presses the point one step further and asks the source of the communal rules themselves, one is thrown back upon all sorts of mythical explanations. Note finally that in all I have said, what constitutes a proper analysis of Being's transcendental priority remains an unresolved question.

For Heidegger an act of understanding constitutes one's situation. The act is transcendentally prior to man. Through it man comes into being *as* man. I now put this point in a way which connects it with what has gone before. I hold the position correct, but not its reference to the concept of understanding. Being is a happening, an act in the broad Aristotelian sense of the term. This act is akin to something living, emerging, and enduring. It is not itself an entity, but it happens only with respect to entities and happens with respect to every entity. In particular and in a primary sense

87. This position is adumbrated in statements such as 'Being gives itself.' This position is presented rather oracularly in Heidegger's later writings.

88. In this connection, see PI. For a critique of the position—perhaps more an expansion of the view than a critique—see Sellars, *Science, Perception and Reality*, pp. 127 ff.

it happens to man. In this way man comes into being as man. In short, through the transcendental happening that is Being man is endowed with his Being: mediated reflexivity. Man is the primary object of Being's happening for obvious reasons. Mediated reflexivity (one's world$_H$) makes possible an awareness of oneself and other entities. In other words, as the structure of awareness it makes awareness itself functionally possible. The concept of awareness is presupposed by and thus necessary to the conceptual framework of functions. Function, like rule, is an intentional notion, whose status is fundamentally conceptual. Thus only through Being's transcendental conferral of itself upon that entity which, through this conferral, comes to be man do entities other than man come to have functional status. Through this mediated conferral of functional status upon nonhuman entities, mediated reflexivity, as the structure of awareness, is at the same time granted access to these entities. This access in its functional dimensions, along with the nonhuman entities functionally revealed, gets expressed in language. Finally, to say that the "object" to which Being happens is indirect, that Being's "object" must appear grammatically in the dative case, is to make this point: reality as *intelligible* exerts no direct causal influence on man as intelligent. More generally, the transcendental relation of intelligibility to intelligence must be construed in other than causal terms, for the concept of causality is foreign to the conceptual framework of intentional modes of behavior

For Heidegger, an act of understanding, transcendentally prior to man, projects a fundamental function. This function is laid before a "prehuman" entity. In terms of this function the entity comes to be aware of itself. This nontotal reflexivity is mediated, however, not only by the function understanding provides, but also by various functions belonging to other entities, namely, those from which a prehuman entity distinguishes itself and in relation to which it becomes aware of itself. The reflexivity of man's awareness, thus, is doubly mediated.

Heidegger holds that understanding results in the creation of a human world (a world$_H$).[89] Revealed immediately by moods, this

89. SZ g.142 ff., e.182 ff. See especially g.144–45, e.184.

world is constituted as a set of functional concepts which is co-terminus with the λογος and thus ultimately identifiable with Being itself. Heidegger's account of how human worlds come to be, however, is problematic. If one's world has transcendental status, accounts of how it comes to be are beyond the domain of strictly phenomenological inquiry. Phenomenologists who undertake such inquiry fall prey to the same objections they level against the constructivistic, speculative excursion into a priori psychology presented by Kant in his first edition transcendental deduction in the *Critique of Pure Reason.*

For Heidegger, the manner in which one relates to the function which first constitutes one's world and the manner in which one is aware of one's world itself determine the way in which entities within one's world are experienced. In short, they determine how entities are interpreted. The two determining factors are not independent of one another. In Heidegger's view the manner in which one relates to the function which first constitutes one's world determines in large measure one's awareness of one's world, and thus it determines most fundamentally one's experience of entities within one's world.[90] One of the results of relating improperly to this function is that the functional characteristics of entities are not perspicuously grasped. Entities are experienced as if they were deficient in functional attributes and functional interrelations. If on the other hand one relates to the world-constituting function properly, entities are revealed perspicuously, that is, in their functional attributes and interrelations, which Heidegger terms their readiness-to-hand.[91]

A perspicuous grasp of entities, thus, not to mention knowledge of oneself, depends upon the *mode* of one's mediated reflexivity, the manner in which one relates to a fundamental function of oneself. Not only this, perspicuity depends also upon the manner in which one is aware of one's world in its mediating influence, and the quality of that world itself. Such is Heidegger's view.

This view raises important questions, the validity of which is

90. In this connection, see SZ g.267 ff., e.312 ff. See also g.252 ff., e.296 ff.

91. Clearly this is a matter of interpretation. See the preceding footnotes.

independent of Heidegger's (mostly nonexistent) answers to them. What *is* a (human) world? Like its predecessors, this question unpacks into a number of closely related questions: What structures constitute a (human) world$_H$? What are a (human) world$_H$'s extracognitive dimensions? How do these dimensions relate to the cognitive dimensions of a (human) world$_H$? How do a (human) world$_H$'s extracognitive dimensions function in its *dialectical*[92] structure? What is the most perspicuous description of a (human) world$_H$'s dialectical structure? How central is the concept of a fundamental function to a dialectical model of a (human) world$_H$? What are the precise conceptual relations which connect a (human) world$_H$ to the person whose world$_H$ it is? By what means are extraphenomenological questions concerning a (human) world$_H$—questions which violate the transcendental principle—to be dealt with?

I am now in a position to bring this study to its end. I have indicated those areas which require redirected exploration and on what foundations these explorations ought to be conducted by formulating questions that constitute a gestalt to which I provisionally apply the term 'man.' Foundations such as these are sturdy, I believe, not only in the way in which man himself is sturdy, but in the way man's most dialectical product, philosophy, is sturdy as well. The foundations invite questions which bring them into question —not all at once, but on that piecemeal basis which constitutes conceptually the development of human intelligence and insight, and historically the unfolding of human civilization. The business of philosophy is almost as diverse as the philosophers who pursue it. One of its tasks, its most central one and the one most relevant to the human situation, is the disciplined articulation of those structures unavoidably constitutive of man and of the questions man asks concerning himself. It has been the goal of this book to aid in the process of this articulation.

92. That the structure of a (human) world$_H$ is dialectical should be obvious from the considerations of this chapter. For a further exploration of the concept of the dialectical, see my "Worlds and World Views," *Man and World* 2:228–47.

Index

Agency, 91, 105, 106, 119, 124, 152–56 passim

Anxiety, 145–46

Appearance, 81, 82, 83

Aristotle, 7, 13 n., 18, 55, 133, 159

Articulation, 54–56 passim, 105, 107

Assertion, 116–17

Attention, 87

Austin, J. L., 2, 14, 15, 15 n., 18, 19, 82, 82 n., 96

Authenticity, 87

Awareness, 87, 91, 104, 109, 113, 124, 130, 155, 156, 160, 161

Baumgarten, Alexander, 85, 87

Being: Heidegger on, 3, 5, 5 n., 13, 22, 24, 44 ff.; considered linguistically, 39, 40, 42, 100–01

Being-in-the-world, 142, 143

Bernstein, Richard, 111 n., 114 n., 115 n.

Bradley, F. H., 28

Brentano, Franz, 67

Carnap, Rudolf, 25 n., 46

Circumstances, 151–53

Cobb, John B., 51 n.

Concepts, 27–28, 155: Wittgenstein on, 110; Sellars on, 111

Consciousness, 67–68, 70, 135, 158, 159

Copula, 14, 21, 22, 24

Dasein, 5 n., 29, 47–53 passim, 96, 105, 116, 127–37 passim, 140–45 passim, 148, 153: definition of, 133

Demske, James, 103 n.

Descartes, René, 26, 48 n., 133–34

Deviation, 9–10

Disclosure, 48, 49, 50, 53, 105, 106–07, 113, 140, 141, 148

Discourse, 98: as intelligibility-articulation, 98–101 passim, 105, 107, 109, 115, 118, 139, 149, 150

Empiricism, 64

Entity, 14, 18, 21, 25, 31–38 passim, 41, 46, 52, 54 ff., 85, 89–92 passim, 98, 106, 133, 138, 143–44, 146, 154–61 passim

Essence, 69, 73, 74

Etymology, 14, 15, 18–20 passim, 21, 22–25, 32, 96

Existentials, 130

Experience, 38, 69, 72, 82, 92, 136, 141, 148, 152, 154, 161: Wittgenstein on, 111

Extralinguistic meaning, 38–39, 44, 100, 119–20

Fact, Heidegger on, 100

Farber, Marvin, 71 n.

Fichte, Johann, 71 n.

Flew, Antony, 27 n.

Fogelin, Robert, 111 n.

Formal mode of speech, 28, 28 n., 46

Forms of life, 110–11

Frege, Gottlob, 64, 67

Freud, Sigmund, 125

Fromm, Erich, 141 n.

Function, 76–79, 118, 119, 156, 161

Geiger, Moritz, 74

Grammar, 16, 17, 26, 32, 34–38
    passim, 64, 65, 68, 100
Grounding, 123

Happening, 7, 31, 37, 49, 77, 78,
    113, 159
Hegel, G. W. F., 12, 12 n., 53, 54,
    54 n., 55, 71 n., 149, 149 n.
Heidegger, Martin: reversal of
    views, 102, 103, 103 n., 104
Herz, Marcus, 86
Hume, David, 26, 66
Husserl, Edmund, 29, 55, 65, 67,
    68, 69, 71, 72, 72 n., 73 n., 74,
    76, 84, 92, 134

Idealism, 88, 94, 100, 149
Ideality, 69
Infinitive, 6–13, 25: metalinguistic
    function, 14
Intentionality, 54, 68, 96–97, 135,
    146, 157, 158, 159, 160: of lan-
    guage, 100, 107, 110, 111

Judgment, 26–28

Kant, Immanuel, 18, 18 n., 27, 27
    n., 28, 38, 71, 71 n., 72, 84, 85,
    86, 89, 89 n., 90, 91, 92, 94, 99,
    122, 130, 132, 134, 135–36, 137,
    143, 146, 149, 154: categories,
    28; experience of entities, 55;
    judgment, 26
Kierkegaard, Sören, 87
Knowledge, 27, 72; empirical, 64

Labeling: Wittgenstein on, 109;
    Heidegger on, 109
Language, 8 ff., 26 n., 41, 42, 44,
    57 ff., 92, 94 ff., 155: Heidegger
    on, 2, 39, 80 ff., 99–101, 103,
    105, 116, 121; Greek, 7, 8, 9, 11,
    13, 16, 19, 20, 20 n., 95, 98;
    language games, 8, 77, 108–11
    passim, 116, 117, 125, 160; Kant
    on, 27; Ryle on, 57 ff.; relation to
    meaning, 105 ff.; Wittgenstein

on, 108–12 passim, 114–15; per-
    spicuous language, 115, 115 n.;
    poetic language, 124–25, 124 n.
Leibniz, Gottfried, 30, 71, 71 n., 91
Logic, 63, 64, 65, 67: of language,
    114
Logos, 98, 99, 101, 105, 109, 149,
    150, 161

Material mode of speech, 25, 45, 100
Meaning, 44 ff., 78, 104, 119: Hei-
    degger on, 2, 21, 112–13, 118–
    19; denotationist view of, 57–60,
    62, 65; monoscopic (meaning),
    59 ff.; connotationist view of, 60;
    functionalist view of, 61 ff. 76 ff.,
    79; ing doctrine, 105, 106; ed
    doctrine, 105, 106; Wittgenstein
    on, 108 ff., 119
Mechanism of sense, 111, 111 n.,
    115
Mediated reflexivity, 104, 113, 134–
    39 passim, 142–45 passim, 149,
    150, 156, 160, 161
Meinong, Alexius, 62, 68
Merleau-Ponty, Maurice, 2, 39, 69,
    70 n., 82, 158, 158 n.
Metaphor, 50, 122
Metaphysics, 85, 86, 87–88
Mill, John Stuart, 57–61 passim, 63,
    67
Modus infinitivus, 6, 9, 10, 21
Moods, 142, 143, 145, 146–47, 149,
    150, 160

Naming, 108, 109
Newton, Isaac, 135, 136, 137, 138
Nietzsche, Friedrich, 12, 87, 151
Nominalist tradition, 69
Nothing, the, 146

Ontic, 33, 37, 86, 89, 136, 137, 144
Ontological, 37, 89, 136, 137, 140,
    148, 153
Ostensive teaching, 109, 110–11,
    117

Participles, 25, 26, 32, 33, 34, 35, 36
Peirce, Charles S., 157–58, 158 n., 159
Pfänder, Alexander, 74
Phenomenology, 2, 30, 38–39, 44, 45, 65, 66, 67, 69, 74–76, 85, 86, 100, 108, 120, 125, 133, 146, 149, 161: phenomenological method, 71 ff., 80 ff.; Heidegger's use of, 87, 101–04; role of language in, 121; positivistic aspect of, 149
Phenomenon, 81–85, 86, 87, 90, 92–96 passim, 99
Philosophy, 8, 9, 11, 13, 71, 123: analytic, 39, 44, 58 ff., 66, 68, 76, 100, 106, 119, 120, 158; continental, 39
Plato, 12 n., 66, 67, 68, 69, 70, 73, 76, 77
Presence, 70, 91–92, 99, 105, 106, 123, 125
Psychology, 67, 75, 141, 154, 161; associationalist, 79, 154
Purpose, 155, 156

Reality, 40, 41, 42
Reason, 54
Reference relationship, 83
Referential opacity, 58
Reflexive analysis, 134, 134 n.
Regularity, 158
Reinach, Adolf, 74
Richardson, W. J., 88 n., 93 n., 98 n., 102 n., 104 n., 143 n., 144 n.
Robinson, James M., 51 n.
Rule, 158, 159
Russell, Bertrand, 63, 65, 67
Ryle, Gilbert, 3, 57, 57 n., 58, 60–68

Sartre, Jean-Paul, 101, 151 n.
Schmitt, Richard, 71 n., 101 n.

Science, 73, 74, 153, 155, 157, 158
Seinsfrage, 5 passim
Sellars, Wilfred, 2, 82 n., 112, 115, 115 n., 156–57, 157 n., 159 n.
Semblance, 81, 82
Signification, 54, 107: Wittgenstein on, 108; Heidegger on, 109, 116
Situation, 104, 105, 150–51, 156
Space, 89–91, 122–23
Spiegelberg, Herbert, 73 n., 84 n., 92 n.
State-of-mind, 139, 140, 142, 150
Strawson, P. F., 148 n.
Syncategorematic terms, 60, 63, 64

Thévanez, Pierre, 134 n.
Thing-in-itself, 84, 85
Thrownness, 140
Time, 18, 33, 123–24, 132: primordial time, 124
Training, 109–11 passim
Transcendental apperception, 137

Underhill, Evelyn, 30 n.

Verbal substantive, 6–12 passim, 25
Vycinas, Vincent, 12 n., 98 n.

Wahl, Jean, 69
Waismann, Friedrich, 40–42, 100 n., 101
Wild, John, 83 n., 85 n., 87, 89 n., 92 n., 123 n.
Wittgenstein, Ludwig, 2, 3, 8, 26 n., 28, 29, 64, 65, 66, 77, 81, 87, 101, 102, 108 n., 108–12, 114, 115, 116, 117–19, 121, 121 n., 147, 147 n., 148, 149, 154, 155, 159: change in, 111–12
Word, 8, 14, 15, 59, 95, 96, 109
World, 88 ff., 97, 125, 140, 147, 150, 162: Heidegger on, 100, 104, 127 ff., 140, 145, 160–61; Wittgenstein on, 115